Footprint Handbook
El Salvador

RICHARD ARGHIRIS

This is
El Salvador

El Salvador is a lively country and the people are just as friendly – some say more so – than in the rest of Central America. Ornately painted and colourful buses bump from place to place, just as they do in Guatemala and Honduras, but El Salvador has better roads and the quality of the buses is superior to that of neighbouring countries. While the rest of Central America relies on tortillas, Salvadoreans fill them with beans, cheese or meat and call them *pupusas*. Pinning it down is difficult but there's a slightly different feel here from neighbouring countries.

Guidebooks tend to urge caution, but in reality El Salvador is no more dangerous than other Central American countries. During the civil war, Salvadoreans sought refuge abroad; now they're returning, bringing with them a gang culture and other less-than-favourable imports from the United States, although as a tourist you are rarely subjected to any of these social problems. Despite the high rate of gang-related crime, frequent natural disasters and a tourist infrastructure less developed than its neighbouring countries, there are some compelling reasons why you should visit El Salvador: dramatic volcanic landscapes, blue-green lagoons, horizon-filling panoramas and golden beaches. In the northern hills around El Poy and Perquín the trekking is divine, with far-reaching views across staggered horizons. The stark cinder cone of Volcán Izalco offers a challenging but rewarding trek from the slopes of Cerro Verde, while El Imposible National Park provides the chance to visit a forest. Along the coast, choose from surfing, diving or simply lazing around and watching the endless display of Pacific sunsets.

Richard Arghiris

Best of
El Salvador

top things to do and see

❶ Puerta del Diablo

The commanding views through the 'Devil's Door' – a natural portal formed by two giant steep slabs of rock – encompass the urban sprawl of the capital San Salvador, the numinous peak of San Vicente volcano and, on a very clear day, the Pacific ocean. Page 28.

❷ Ruta de las Flores

Soak up the warmth, colour and disarming rural charm on the Ruta de las Flores ('Route of the Flowers'). The procession of cobblestone towns and villages are alive with colour and colonial beauty. Aromatic coffee fincas, gastronomic fairs, local arts and crafts, and bucolic highland scenery are among the attractions in the area. Page 42.

❸ Joya de Cerén

Dubbed the 'Pompeii of the Americas', the ancient farming community of Joya de Cerén was buried under 14 layers of volcanic ash around the year 590 AD, perfectly preserving it until its accidental discovery in 1976. Today, this UNESCO World Heritage Site continues to be excavated and offers an intimate glimpse of daily Mayan life. Page 51.

❹ Cerro Verde

The lost world volcanic landscapes of the Cerro Verde National Park – one of El Salvador's finest natural attractions – include the massive crater lake of Lago Coatepeque and no less than three volcanic cones: Cerro Verde, Izalco and Santa Ana. There is also some great trekking, wildlife and flowers. Page 52.

❺ El Zonte, Tunco and Sunzal beaches

Pounded by world class surf, the black sand beaches of El Salvador's Pacific coast have long been sought out by intrepid waveseekers. In recent years, the emergence of low-key resorts and bohemian party towns are drawing a new sort of traveller to the region. Page 64.

❻ Parque Nacional El Imposible

Named for its perilous ravines and generally challenging terrain, the so-called 'Impossible' National Park is a wonderland of primeval forests and exotic wildlife, the most biodiverse place in El Salvador. It's worth the extra effort to get to this remote and special wilderness. Page 65.

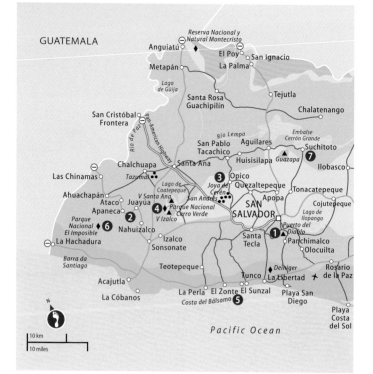

➐ Suchitoto

On the shore of the expansive Suchitlán lake, the well-to-do colonial town of Suchitoto is regarded as the cultural capital of El Salvador. Its traditional good looks, tranquil airs and emphasis on the arts are fuelling its popularity and renaissance, and make it a must-see in the northern region of the country. Page 71.

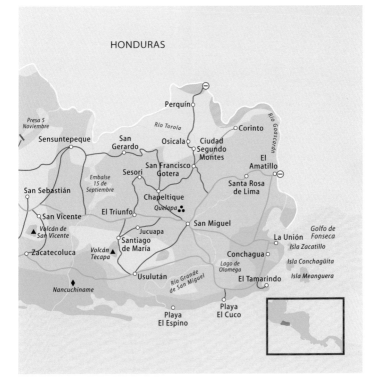

HONDURAS

Presa 5 Noviembre

Perquín

Río Torola

Corinto

Sensuntepeque

San Gerardo

Osicala

Ciudad Segundo Montes

El Amatillo

San Francisco Gotera

Río Goascorán

Sesori

Santa Rosa de Lima

San Sebastián

Embalse 15 de Septiembre

Chapeltique

Quelapa

San Vicente

El Triunfo

Volcán de San Vicente

Jucuapa

San Miguel

La Unión

Golfo de Fonseca

Zacatecoluca

Volcán Tecapa

Santiago de María

Conchagua

Isla Zacatillo

Isla Conchagüita

Nancuchiname

Usulután

Río Grande de San Miguel

Lago de Olomega

El Tamarindo

Isla Meanguera

Playa El Espino

Playa El Cuco

Volcano Usulatan

Route planner

El Salvador is subtly different to the other Central American nations. You could shoot through the main highlights in 10 days or else hang out for two to three weeks and soak up the nuances; if you've got the time, you'll enjoy the difference. With so many crossings and borders, the options for travel in and around El Salvador are very flexible. Points of interest are spread throughout the country so there is no natural route to travel. In some parts of the country the infrastructure for tourism is quite rudimentary, but in others (such as the capital and nearby places of interest and some of the beach resorts) it is well developed.

Life in El Salvador focuses strongly on San Salvador. All roads lead towards the capital with just a few exceptions. Planning your trip will involve either a visit to San Salvador or at least travelling through it. Fortunately the country is so small that the capital can make a convenient base, thus avoiding the hassle of dragging your bags across the country.

One week to ten days
volcanoes and colonial towns

Worth a day's visit, **San Salvador** is a cosmopolitan city with a variety of architectural styles that have been created by the multitude of rebuilding projects in a history dogged by earthquakes. The city centre is always busy and widely thought of as unsafe at night, so newcomers are best advised to head for the western areas around Boulevard de los Héroes, with its shopping malls and restaurants, and the residential districts of Escalón and the Zona Rosa with its major shopping malls with fancy stores, branded boutiques and restaurants and nightclubs.

Throughout El Salvador volcanoes dominate the landscape, and the scenery is one of its main attractions. Just south of the capital, and easily accessible from the city centre by bus, **Parque Balboa** has fine views of Volcán San Vicente through the dramatic Puerta del Diablo (Devil's Door) and from the Mirador in the centre of the mountain village of **Los Planes de Renderos**.

A short distance west of San Salvador you can do a day trip to the country's main archaeological sites of **San Andrés** and the **Joya de Cerén**, where a Maya settlement has been preserved under volcanic ash. There are no grand temples and sculptures, but the dwellings and everyday objects found here are the only ones of their type preserved from the Maya era in Central America.

Just west of the Joya de Cerén, **Parque Nacional Cerro Verde** is a good spot to explore for a few days, with its prospect over Izalco and Santa Ana volcanoes and the deep-blue waters of the beautiful **Lago de Coatepeque**. Closed for two years after earthquakes, Cerro Verde recuperated its unique flora and fauna, was declared a protected natural area and is now open to foreign visitors.

Southwest of Parque Nacional Cerro Verde is the **Ruta de las Flores**, a handful of villages climbing the volcanic chains with good scenery and waterfalls, pleasant hiking and a smattering of crafts. It's worth taking a day or two to travel along some of this route by bus or car, starting at the interesting town of **Sonsonate**.

After the Ruta de las Flores, you could either head further west still, towards the Guatemalan border, to the **Parque Nacional El Imposible**, one of the largest national parks in Central America, or south to the Pacific towns of **Tunco**, **El Sunzal** and **El Zonte** on the Costa del Bálsamo. These places have great surf and black sand beaches and make a good spot to kick back for a few days before returning to San Salvador.

Three weeks or more

archaeological sites and surfing

With more time, you could visit the places mentioned above at a more leisurely pace and explore the surrounding areas. Take a few days in San Salvador to take trips to nearby places like **Cihuatán**, El Salvador's largest archaeological park and the largest city in Mesoamerica at the time of the Toltecs, north of the centre, or Parque Balboa to the south. **Panchimalco** is an old village south of the capital where cultural traditions are kept alive by a growing handicraft industry. The community hosts the yearly Procesión de Las Palmas, a spectacular floral procession in the beginning of May.

The Pacific coast at **La Libertad** is only a short trip south from San Salvador and is a good place to start exploring the Balsam coast to the west, the surfing beaches and to get a feel for the country as a whole. East of La Libertad, the beaches of the **Costa del Sol** are definitely worth a stop for a few days for their long stretches of sand and estuaries. Further east of the Costa del Sol is the

Golfo de Fonseca with secluded beaches which you can explore. From the port of La Unión, you can take a boat to the islands in the gulf. It's just a short trip from here to the Nicaraguan border at El Amatillo.

Inland from the Costa del Sol is the city of **San Vicente**, with an impressive volcano nearby, and the transport hub of **San Miguel,** as well as many small traditional towns. Those interested in the recent civil war can visit **Perquín**, north of San Miguel near the Honduran border. From Perquín it's easy to cross the border for Gracias or Tegucigalpa in Honduras.

Heading west from San Salvador, after exploring the Parque Nacional Cerro Verde, you could stay in **Santa Ana**, a good base for visiting the archaeological sites of **Tazumal** and **Casa Blanca**. There are very few pockets of undisturbed land in the country, mainly because El Salvador is farmed intensively. On the border with Guatemala and Honduras, however, is **Montecristo**, a remnant of cloudforest administered jointly by the three countries. You can reach Montecristo from Santa Ana via Metapán and it's worth staying the night so you can hike to the summit.

Returning to Metapán, you can then head east towards vast Cerrón Grande reservoir, set in beautiful scenery. On its shores is **Suchitoto**, one of the best preserved colonial towns in the country, and currently enjoying a revival. Northwest of Cerrón Grande, near the Honduran border, are the towns of **La Palma** and **San Ignacio**, where handicrafts of brightly painted wood and other styles are made. If you're going to Honduras, head to the border town of **El Poy**, north of San Ignacio, if you want to drop into Santa Rosa de Copán.

When to go

The most pleasant months are from November to January. El Salvador is fortunate in that temperatures are rarely excessively high. March to May are the hottest months; December to February the coolest. There is one rainy season, from May to October, with April and November being transitional periods; there are only light rains for the rest of the year. Highest temperatures and humidity will be found on the coast and in the lowlands, with the heat at its greatest from March to May.

Weather San Salvador

January	February	March	April	May	June
18°C 28°C 10mm	18°C 29°C 0mm	19°C 30°C 10mm	21°C 30°C 30mm	21°C 28°C 130mm	21°C 27°C 310mm

July	August	September	October	November	December
20°C 28°C 280mm	20°C 28°C 330mm	20°C 27°C 330mm	20°C 27°C 210mm	19°C 27°C 30mm	18°C 27°C 0mm

What to do

from archaeology to surfing

Archaeology and architecture

El Salvador played host to Mesoamerican civilization in its earliest phases. Near Santa Tecla, the site of Joya de Cerén is the only known Mayan settlement to have been perfectly preserved in volcanic ash, offering unique insights into the region's pre-Hispanic way of life. Outside the city of Santa Ana, Tazumal is the largest excavated ruin in the country and features a large pyramid. Nearby, the pre-Classic site of Casa Blanca shows architectural influence from Central Mexico. The country's colonial heritage is very well-preserved in a number of atmospheric towns and villages and Suchitoto is the big highlight. Ciudad Vieja, 10 km south of Suchitoto, was the first location of San Salvador and is currently on the UNESCO World Heritage tentative list.

Birdwatching and wildlife observation

El Salvador does not embrace 2 coastlines like most of its Central American siblings, but it is still highly biodiverse thanks to its dramatic contrast of highlands and lowlands. In total, the country harbous some 1477 species of vertebrates, including threatened species such as the puma and harpy eagle. Any of its protected areas offer the opportunity to glimpse wildlife (see Hiking below), but the Parque Nacional El Imposible is the

ON THE ROAD
Shopping

The best place to buy arts and crafts is in the village where the items are originally made; Ilobasco for ceramics, San Sebastián for hammocks and La Palma for painted wooden boxes, Nahuizalco for baskets and furniture of wicker and jute. If you cannot go there in person, the markets in San Salvador (the Mercado Ex-Cuartel and Mercado de Artesanía) sell many of these items at slightly higher prices. Branches of Nahanché have outlets in the major shopping malls with good quality handicrafts from all over the country.

best. Generally, birding is not as spectacular as neighbouring Honduras owing to far fewer forests, but with 583 species of avifauna, El Salvador can more than satisfy most ardent twitchers. The national bird is the turquoise-browed Motmot.

Hiking

Filled with scenes of bucolic tranquillity, the hills and plantations on the Ruta de las Flores are good for casual rambling, as is the countryside around Suchitoto and Perquín, both popular staging posts for outdoor adventures. Challenging jungles treks can be had in the Parque Nacional El Imposible, the largest and most geographically diverse protected area in El Salvador. In the north, the country's only cloudforests can be explored in the Parque Nacional Montecristo; if you're lucky, you might glimpse a quetzal. Volcano trekkers should head to the Parque Nacional Cerro Verde where three different cones invite exploration.

Surfing

West of La Libertad, the Costa del Bálsamo harbours a procession of epic surf spots. The best is Punta Roca, a legendary world class break that is surprisingly uncrowded. Development throughout the region has been consistent but mercifully low-key; everything from rustic beach huts to boutique surf lodges are available.

Where to stay

As the most industrialized of the Central American states El Salvador has an impressive selection of international-standard business hotels in San Salvador. The country also has a good selection of more expensive hotels for those taking weekend breaks from the capital. At the lower end there is no shortage of cheap accommodation, but there is a shortage of good, cheap places to stay. If you have the time, shop around and don't check into the first hotel you come to. If travelling at holiday times, book accommodation in advance.

Price codes

Where to stay		Restaurants	
$$$$	over US$150	$$$	over US$12
$$$	US$66-150	$$	US$7-12
$$	US$30-65	$	US$6 and under
$	under US$30		

Price of a double room in high season, including taxes.

Prices for a two-course meal for one person, excluding drinks or service charge.

Food
& drink

Food

Pupusas, stuffed tortillas made of corn or ricemeal, are the quintessential Salvadorean dish. They come in several varieties including *chicharrón* (pork crackling), *queso* (cheese) and *revueltas* (mixed), and are typical, tasty and cheap. The ones sold at street stalls are better there than at restaurants, but beware of stomach infection from the accompanying *curtido* (pickled cabbage). On Saturday and Sunday nights people congregate in *pupuserías*. *Pavo* (turkey) is common and good, as are *frijoles* (red beans). A *boca* is an appetizer, a small dish of yucca, avocado or chorizo, served with a drink before a meal. Apart from in San Salvador, restaurants tend to close early, around 2000.

Drink

Coffee makes an excellent souvenir and is good value and delicious. For beer, light lagers are the norm, as elsewhere in Central America; Suprema is stronger than Pilsener, while Golden Light is a reduced-alcohol beer.

Chicha is a traditional alcoholic drink made from corn, sometimes with a trace of pineapple; El Salvador also has a stronger, distilled version called *chaparro*. Although illegal to sell, everyone has their source. When made well *chicha* can taste similar to white wine. It is a trademark of the Maya and is particularly well made in the western village of Izalco. Ask at the tourist office there for a *chicha* contact to purchase a sample. *Chaparro curado* contains fruit or honey. It is a favourite at election times when alcohol sales are banned. Water bottles are emptied and filled with the clear *chaparro* for illegal swigging on the streets.

Essential San Salvador

Finding your feet

Four broad streets meet at the city centre: Avenida Cuscatlán and its continuation Avenida España run south to north; Calle Delgado and its continuation Calle Arce, with a slight blip, from east to west. This principle is retained throughout: the *avenidas* run north to south and the *calles* east to west. The even-numbered *avenidas* are east of the central *avenidas*, odd numbers west; north of the central *calles*, they are dubbed Norte, south of the central *calles* Sur. The even-numbered *calles* are south of the two central *calles*, the odd numbers north. East of the central *avenidas* they are dubbed Oriente (Ote), west of the central *avenidas* Poniente (Pte). Sounding more complicated than it is, the system is straightforward and quickly grasped.

Best restaurants

Café Café, page 32
La Hola Beto's Escalón, page 32
La Hacienda Real, page 32
Kalpataru, page 33
Rustico Bistro, page 33

Getting around

The main focal points of the city are the historical centre, the commercial district some 3 km to the west around Boulevard de los Héroes, and the residential and commercial districts of Escalón and Zona Rosa another 2 km further west. City buses and taxis are needed to get between the three (see page 36).

Safety

The city centre is considered by many to be dangerous after dark. San Benito, Maquilishuat, La Gran Via and Multiplaza are considered safer areas than others, but you should still take care. As a general rule, stay out of poorly lit areas and keep to main roads where there are more people around. At night, taxis are strongly recommended if you don't know exactly where you're going.

Armed security personnel are commonplace. There is a heightened atmosphere of tension in some areas. In downtown areas, especially at markets, don't carry cameras, wear watches or jewellery, or flash money around. Be vigilant when withdrawing cash from ATMs. See also www.gov.uk/foreign-travel-advice/el-salvador.

Pollution

Since it is in a hollow, the city has a very bad smog problem, caused mainly by traffic pollution. Efforts are being made to reduce vehicle emissions.

When to go

The climate is semi-tropical. The average for San Salvador is 28°C with a variation of only about 3°C. Days are often hot, especially in the dry season, but the temperature drops in the late afternoon and nights are usually pleasantly mild. See also the weather chart on page 12.

San Salvador
& around

Surrounded by a ring of mountains in a highly seismic valley known as 'Valle de las Hamacas', San Salvador toils under the threat of earthquakes. As one of the largest cities in Central America, a sprawling, relentless and busy place, San Salvador can at times seem almost heartless. Do not be deceived. Beneath its hard urban exterior are some sensitive cultural inclinations and a slew of intriguing museums dedicated to art, anthropology and history. There are green zones too, including city parks, a botanical garden and a zoo. San Salvador also retains the charm of the Spanish era, thanks to being one of the first European cities in the New World.

From the nouveau riche to the urban poor, its human geography is framed by its great wealth disparities. In the downtown area, crumbling buildings await renovation and restoration. More prosperous neighbourhoods to the west have since risen to glory, with their gleaming shopping malls and designer suburbs.

Beyond the outskirts, western El Salvador is a verdant, compact and easy to explore region with good transport links. It combines the dramatic volcanic landscapes of Cerro Verde, Volcán Izalco and Lago de Coatepeque with the serene beauty of highland communities along the colourful Ruta de las Flores. On the Pacific coast are a string of low-key resorts and surf towns.

Centro Histórico

a rich blend of architectural styles and underrated cultural attractions

The Centro Histórico in San Salvador (altitude 680-1000 m, population 2,297,282 including suburbs) is laid out in a classic colonial grid but few colonial buildings have survived history's devastating tremors. Instead, the downtown core is complemented by a trove of fascinating 20th-century architecture: art deco, futurist, neo-gothic, modernist and populuxe works are all on display.

① San Salvador

Where to stay	Hostal Doña Marta 5	Villa del Angel 11
Aparthotel María José 1	Joan's Hostel 6	
Arbol de Fuego	Las Magnolias 7	**Restaurants**
Eco-hotel 2	Posada del Angel 8	Al Pomodoro 1
Casa ILB il Bongustaio 3	Real Intercontinental	Automariscos 2
Hostal Cumbres	San Salvador 9	Café Café 3
del Volcán 4	Tazumal House 10	El Bodegón 4

At the intersection of Avenida Cuscatlán and Calle Rubén Darío is the **Plaza Barrios**, the heart of the Centro Histórico. A fine equestrian statue looks west towards the renaissance-style **Palacio Nacional** ① *Mon-Fri 0800-1600, free.* Built 1904-1911 to replace an earlier structure, it contains a wealth of antique furnishings spread across 105 rooms and four main salons in red, yellow, pink and blue.

To the north is the **Catedral Metropolitana**, which was left unfinished for several years after Archbishop Romero suspended its construction to use the money to reduce poverty. Work was resumed in 1990 and completed in 1999,

> ➡ **San Salvador maps**
> 1 San Salvador, page 22
> 2 San Salvador centre, page 24

El Sopón Típico **5**
Kalpataru **6**
Kamakura **7**
Kreef **8**
La Hacienda Real **9**
La Hola Beto's Escalón **10**
La Panetière **11**

Mercadito Merliot **12**
Rustico Bistro **13**
Shaw's **14**
Zócalo Escalón **15**

Bars & clubs 🎵
Café La T **16**
El Arpa (Bar Irlandés) **17**
La Luna **18**
Photo Café **19**

the last consecration of a cathedral of the millennium. It now stands as a beacon of tranquillity amid the dirt and noise of the downtown capital. It commands a striking presence, gleaming white and modern, its façade flanked by two giant murals vividly splashed with the colourful work of the country's most famous artist, **Fernando Llort**. Inside it is quite bare, but for the fabulous circular stained-glass window of a dove surrounded by a hundred shards of brilliant yellow glass, which in turn is framed by yellow stars set in deep lapis lazuli-blue glass. Beneath the cathedral, a new chapel has been created to house the tomb of assassinated **Archbishop Oscar Romero**.

Two blocks east of Plaza Barrios is **Parque Libertad** with the rebuilt church of **El Rosario** on the eastern side where José Matías Delgado, father of the Independence movement, lies buried. The interior, decked out in modern sculpture, is fascinating and well worth a visit; go early morning or late afternoon to see the stunning light effect of the modern stained-glass window. The **Palacio Arquiepiscopal** is next door. Not far away to the southeast, on 10 Avenida Sur, is another rebuilt church, **La Merced**, whose belltower rang out Father Delgado's tocsin call to Independence in 1811.

One block north of Plaza Barrios, at the intersection of Calle Delgado and 2a Avenida Sur, is the **Teatro Nacional** ⓘ *Plaza Morazán, T2222-5689*, with a

2 San Salvador centre

monument to General Morazán. The theatre reopened in 2008, after a complete restoration following earthquake damage in 2001; it hosts a regular programme of performances, sometimes free, in a sumptuous auditorium with red velvet seats. Heading east three blocks along Delgado is the **Mercado Ex-Cuartel**, and the expected confusion of sounds and smells that besiege the senses. Nearby are some of the cheapest (and most insalubrious) hotels in the city.

West of the Centro Histórico

commercial district with worthwhile museums, and slick shopping centres and restaurants

Running west from the Teatro Nacional, Calle Delgado changes its name to Calle Arce and passes the great church of El Sagrado Corazón de Jesús on 13 Avenida Norte, worth seeing for its stained-glass windows. Turn left (south) one block and you come to Parque Bolívar, perched between the national printing office and the Department of Health. Running along its north side is Calle Rubén Darío (2a Calle Poniente), which becomes Alameda Roosevelt, then Paseo General Escalón as it leads through the commercial and residential districts west of the centre.

Five blocks west of Parque Bolívar on Alameda Roosevelt is **Parque Cuscatlán** with its green lawns and shady trees, always a hit with families on Sundays. Here you'll find the sombre **Monumento a la Memoria y la Verdad** ⓘ *www.memoriayverdad.org*, which contains the engraved names of 30,000 victims of El Salvador's civil war. For something lighter, head to the **Tin Marín Museo de los Niños** ⓘ *6-10 Calle Pte, entre Gimnasio Nacional y Parque Cuscatlán, www.tinmarin.org, Tue-Sun 0900-1715, US$3*, a colourful children's museum that includes a butterfly reserve and planetarium. Heading north from the park on 25 Avenida Norte takes you in the direction of the University. Turn left at 27 Avenida Norte for the **Museo de la Palara y la Imagen (MUPI)** ⓘ *27 Av Norte 1140, between 19 y 21 Calle Pte, T2564-7005, www.museo.com.sv, Mon-Fri 0800-1200 and 1400-1700, Sat 0800-1200, US$1*. Dedicated to preserving memories of the civil war, its collection includes a movie, photo and audio archive, and a social science library.

Continuing west on Alameda Roosevelt, there is a major junction at 49 Avenida: to the south, the avenue passes the national stadium, **Estadio Olímpico Flor Blanca**, before becoming the main highway to the international airport. To the north, it crosses Alameda Juan Pablo II, beyond which it changes name to **Bulevar de los Héroes**, home to the fashionable shopping centres, **Metrocentro** and the newer **Metrosur**, the **Hotel Real Intercontinental**, some of the city's better restaurants and a glut of fast-food places, which is a busy area at all times, especially at night. At the petrol station by Metrocentro, mariachis and other musicians gather each evening, waiting to be hired; others wander around the restaurants, playing to diners.

The next big landmark on Alameda Roosevelt at the Plaza Las Américas is the **Monumento al Salvador del Mundo**, a statue of Jesus standing on the Earth atop a column. From this junction the Pan-American Highway heads southwest to Santa Tecla. Straight ahead is **Paseo General Escalón**, Parque Beethoven and an area with many restaurants, shops, and the Colonia Escalón residential district. Hidden behind the towering office blocks and flanking the Salvador monument on the southwest is the **Museo Forma** ⓘ *Av Manuel Enrique Araujo, T2298-4269, Mon-Fri 1000-1700, Sat 1000-1300, US$3*, a small modern art gallery housed in a neocolonial-style castle. It hosts an interesting collection of paintings and sculpture by Salvadorean artists.

Zona Rosa and Colonia San Benito
refreshingly leafy residential and entertainment quarters

Accessed from either the Pan-American Highway or Escalón are the **Zona Rosa** and **Colonia San Benito**, home to some of the city's most elegant restaurants and upscale hotels, This area also has many art galleries such as **Galería Espacio** ⓘ *Av La Capilla*, **Galería 1-2-3** ⓘ *Calle La Reforma*, and **La Pinacoteca** ⓘ *Blv Hipódromo*, to name a few. See local press for details of exhibitions.

The **Museo Nacional de Antropología David J Guzman (MUNA)** ⓘ *Feria Internacional, Av de la Revolución y Cra a Santa Tecla, T2243-3750, Tue-Sun 1000-1800, US$3*, is a modern museum worth visiting, showcasing exhibits on the country's archaeological and historical past as well as numerous cultural events; descriptions in Spanish only, but free guided tours available in afternoons with English-speaking guides (check at the desk as they only operate if enough visitors). Just north of the museum at the end of Avenida Revolución is the **Museo de Arte de El Salvador (MARTE)** ⓘ *T2243-6099, www.marte. org.sv, Tue-Sun 1000-1800, US$1.50 (free on Sun), café and shop (both closed Sun) in lobby*. This privately run modern arts museum has permanent exhibits depicting the history of Salvadorean painters with temporary exhibits of artists from Latin America and other parts of the world.

Tip...
Foreigners are advised not to be out in the city centre after dark.

For a refreshing stroll in pleasant landscaped gardens, take the No 44 bus southwest of the Zona Rosa and ask the driver to drop you at the turn-off for the

Jardín Botánico La Laguna ⓘ *Antiguo Cuscatlan, www.jardinbotanico.org.sv, Sat-Sun 0900-1730.*

North of Zona Rosa is **El Arbol de Dios** ⓘ *Av Masferrer 575, opposite Kreef, T2263-9206, www.fernando-llort.com, Mon-Fri 0800-1900, Sat 0900-1800*, an arts and crafts shop, restaurant, museum and garden, operated by the famed Salvadorean artist Fernando Llort, who designed the façade of the Metropolitan Cathedral and is known for his naïf-style wood paintings. The display here also includes the work of other artists.

Around San Salvador

lush hills, bucolic villages and spectacular views

If the crush of humanity become too much in the capital, many places can be visited in a day from San Salvador either on the frequent bus services or by car. There are potential day trips to nearby volcanoes, crater lakes and beauty spots, such as Los Planes de Renderos, the Puerta del Diablo and San Salvador's own volcano, Boquerón, which has a paved road all the way to the top.

To the south is the indigenous village of **Panchimalco**, heading east are the beautiful setting and views around **Lago de Ilopango**; and to the southwest the crater of **Volcán San Salvador** (see page 29). Heading west towards Santa Ana, but still manageable in a day, are the archaeological sites of **Joya de Cerén**, El Salvador's Pompeii, **San Andrés** (see page 51) and the peaks of **Volcán Izalco** and **Cerro Verde** (see page 52) with the deep blue waters of **Lago de Coatepeque** in the crater below.

The limits of a comfortable weekend trip will take you to the garden park of **Ichanmichen**, which is restful (see page 92), and the pyramid of **Tazumal** (west of Santa Ana) is also worth a visit (see page 56). At weekends the coast around La Libertad (see page 61) is very popular. Bus No 495 from the Terminal del Occidente goes to the seaside resort of **Costa del Sol** (see page 91).

South of the Centro Histórico

Lasting most of the day by bus (No 12), or two to three hours by car, a good sightseeing tour heads south of the Centro Histórico. Starting a few blocks southwest of the main square on the eastern side of the Mercado Central, it includes the **San Salvador Zoo** ⓘ *Calle Modelo, T2270-0828, Wed-Sun 0900-1600, US$1*, which, although small, is quiet and attractive. Southeast of the zoo, the **Museo Militar de las Fuerzas Armadas** ⓘ *behind the presidential palace of San Jacinto at the former Cuartel El Zapote, 10 Av Sur y Calle Capitán Alberto Sánchez, T2250-0000, daily 0800-1200 and 1400-1700, free*, has a collection of exhibits of weapons, uniforms and decorations of the armed forces, and weapons captured from FMLN guerrillas. Several blocks away inside Parque Saburo Hirao is the small **Museo de Historia Natural (MUHNES)** ⓘ *Final Calle Los Viveros, Wed-Sun 0900-1600, US$0.75*, with interesting displays on prehistoric findings and a herbal medicine garden. Coninuing south on winding highway RN 6S takes you into a residential district in the mountain range of **Planes de Renderos**. This place is crowned by the beautiful **Parque Balboa** ⓘ *daily 0800-1800, see under Puerta de Diablo below for how to get there*, and there's a good view of the city from El Mirador at the foot of the park. Parque Balboa is a **Turicentro**, with cycle paths, playground and gardens.

★ Puerta del Diablo

Bus No 12 from eastern side of Mercado Central and No 12-MC marked 'Mil Cumbres' run almost hourly to Puerta del Diablo and Parque Balboa. Bus No 17 goes from the same location to Panchimalco through Los Planes de Renderos so you can get off at the junction there and take the No 12 to Parque Puerta del Diablo and Parque Balboa.

From the **Parque Balboa** a scenic road runs to the summit of **Cerro Chulo**, from which the view, seen through the Puerta del Diablo (Devil's Door), is even better.

The Puerta del Diablo consists of two enormous, nearly vertical rocks which frame a magnificent view of the Volcán San Vicente. The rocks are very steep but the sides can be climbed on reasonable paths for an even better view. A little beyond the car park and drinks stands at the Puerta del Diablo is a path climbing up a further summit, from which there are 360-degree views: to the coast, Lago Ilopango, the capital and volcanoes, including San Salvador, Izalco and Cerro Verde and San Vicente.

At the foot of Cerro Chulo is **Panchimalco** (see below). The route to Panchimalco (No 17 from Mercado Central) and the coast branches off the road to Parque Balboa at the village of **Los Planes**, a few kilometres before the park.

Panchimalco

Bus No 17 from Mercado Central at 12 Calle Poniente, San Salvador, every 45 mins (45 mins), or minibus from near Mercado Central, very crowded but quicker (30 mins), and cheaper (US$0.80).

This small town and the surrounding area are home to the **Pancho**, descendants of the Pipil tribes, one of the region's dominant indigenous groups prior to conquest. This is one of the few places in El Salvador where you can still see indigenous people in traditional dress. Streets of large cobbles, with low adobe houses, thread their way between huge boulders at the foot of Cerro Chulo. A very fine baroque colonial church, Santa Cruz, has a white façade with statues of eight saints. Inside are splendid woodcarvings and wooden columns, altars, ceilings and benches. There is a bell inscribed with the cipher and titles of the Holy Roman Emperor Charles V, and a colourful cemetery. The Casa de La Cultura in the main street has frequent cultural events and crafts stores. The **Fiesta de Santa Cruz de Roma** is held on 12-14 September, with music and traditional dances; on 3 May (or the second Sunday of the month) there is the procession of **Las Palmas**.

Lago de Ilopango

Bus No 15, marked Apulo, runs from the bus stop on Parque Hula Hula in San Salvador to the lake (via the airport), 1¼ hrs, US$1. Entrance to the Turicentro camping site costs US$0.60.

Beyond the four-lane highway to Ilopango airport (14.5 km east) lie the deep waters of Lago de Ilopango. Surrounded by mountains, the views around El Salvador's largest and deepest crater lake are impressive. Before the conquest local people used to appease the harvest gods by drowning four virgins here every year. Private chalets make access to the lake difficult, except at clubs and the **Turicentro Apulo**, but it is well worth a visit. The eastern shore is less polluted and is reached from Cojutepeque. There are a number of lakeside cafés and bathing clubs, some of which hire dug-outs by the hour. The cafés are busy in the dry season (try **Teresa's** for fish dishes), but often closed in the middle of the year. Hotel **Vista del Lago** ① *3 km from Apulo turn-off on the highway*, is on a hill top.

Volcán San Salvador
Buses leave a block from Plaza Merliot in San Salvador. By car you turn right just after the Plaza Merliot Mall and continue to the end of the road where a paved road takes you up the volcano.

This large massif at 1839 m has an impressive crater, more than 1.5 km wide and 543 m deep, known as **El Boquerón**. About 2 km to the east is the equally dramatic peak of **El Picacho** (1960 m), which dominates the capital. A walk clockwise round the crater takes about two hours; the first half is easy, the second half rough. The views are magnificent, if somewhat spoilt by TV and radio towers. The area by Boquerón is now a park administrated by the Ministry of Tourism. The area is closed off, with guards during opening hours (daily 0800-1500). **La Laguna** botanical garden is near the summit. The inner slopes of the crater are covered with trees, and at the bottom is a smaller cone from the eruption of 1917.

You can follow the road north and then turn right through extensive coffee plantations and forest to reach the summit of **El Picacho**. This also makes an excellent climb from the Escalón suburb of San Salvador, in the early morning preferably, which takes about three to four hours return trip (take a guide). The easy access, great views and fresh climate has made the Volcán San Salvador a popular destination for people in the capital and, as a result, new restaurants have opened their doors in recent years. See Restaurants, page 31.

Another access to the volcano from the city side is by **Ecoparque El Espino** ① *run by El Espino Cooperative T2289-0749/69, US$1.50*. The entrance is by the Polideportivo in Ciudad Merliot, take bus No 42 Calle especial and walk 100 m. They have several trails, bike rental and small cafeterias. The trails end at a mirador with a panoramic view of the city.

Tourist information

Corporación Salvadoreña de Turismo (Corsatur)
Edif Carbonel No 1, Col Roma Alameda Dr Manuel Enrique Araujo Pasaje Carbonel San Salvador, T2243-7835, www. elsalvador.travel. Mon-Fri 0800-1230 and 1330-1730.
Good information on buses, archaeological sites, beaches and national parks. Texaco and Esso sell good maps at some of their service stations.

Instituto Geográfico Nacional
1 Calle Pte y 43 Av Norte 02310, Col Flor Blanca, T2260-8000.
The best maps of the city and country.

Instituto Salvadoreño de Turismo (ISTU)
41 Av Norte y Alameda Roosevelt 115, T2260-9249, www.istu.gob.sv.
Has useful information about the 13 government-run Turicentros recreation and water parks in the country and on Cerro Verde and Walter T Deininger national parks.

Where to stay

In the downtown area, some hotels lock their doors very early. Many cheap *hospedajes* near Terminal de Oriente are of dubious safety and not recommended for single women. 13% VAT (IVA) is added to bills at major hotels. Most of the cheaper hotels are around the Centro Histórico. Be careful in this area, particularly at night.

$$$$ Casa ILB il Bongustaio
Blv del Hipodromo 605, Colonia San Benito, T2528-4200, www.casailb.com.
This upscale boutique lodging has 5 stylish, contemporary, minimalist suites with crisp tones and generous floor space. Each is equipped with cable TV, Wi-Fi, minibar and plush furnishings. Facilities include a bar, restaurant and parking. An attractive option. Recommended.

$$$$ Hotel Real Intercontinental San Salvador
Blv de los Héroes and Av Sisimiles, in front of the Metrocentro, T2211-3333, www.grupo real.com.
A useful landmark, smart, formal atmosphere (popular with business visitors), **Avis** car hire, **Taca** desk, and a shop selling souvenirs, postcards, US papers and magazines.

$$$ Aparthotel María José
Av La Capilla 223, Zona Rosa, Colonia San Benito, T2263-4790, www.aparthotelmariajose.com.
These cosy, modern apartments have fully equipped kitchens (with fridge, toaster-oven, and coffee machine), dining room, bedroom, and living room with cable TV and sofa bed. Wi-Fi and parking.

$$$ Villa del Angel
71 Av Norte 219, Colonia Escalón, T2223-7171, www.villadelangelhotel.com.
This villa-style guesthouse has simple, modern, minimalist rooms with a trendy lime green colour scheme and all mod cons including super-efficient a/c, Wi-Fi, hot water and cable TV. There's also a small garden. Conveniently located next to Escalón mall.

$$$-$$ Posada del Angel
85 Av Norte 321, Colonia Escalón, T2556-1172, www.hotellaposadadelangel.com.
Featuring tasteful and down-to-earth decor, rooms at the Posada del Angel are quiet, calming and cosy. Breakfast is served in the garden, which is well-maintained with lavish plant life. Good value, accommodating and professionally managed.

$$ Arbol de Fuego Eco-hotel
Av Antiguo Cuscatlan 11C, Colonia La Sultana, T2557-3601, www.arboldefuego.com.
With numerous accolades and international recommendations for its sustainable practices, this attractive eco-hotel offers cosy rooms with typical Salvadoran decor, including locally sourced textiles and artwork, as well as all the usual amenities including Wi-Fi, cable TV, a/c and hot water. An oasis in the urban jungle. Breakfast included. Recommended.

$$ Hotel Tazumal House
Final 35 Av Norte 3, Reparto Santa Fe, T2235-2506, www.hoteltazumalhouse.com.
Located near the university, Tazumal house offers simple, modern, comfortable rooms with all the usual conveniences including cable TV, a/c, Wi-Fi and hot water. There's a pleasant garden out back where you can rest, relax, or take breakfast in the morning. Friendly, homely, hospitable and good value.

$$ Las Magnolias
Av Las Magnolias 226, Col. San Benito, T2528-6500, www.lasmagnolias.com.sv.
This unassuming hotel with 2 wings, old and new, is situated in a quiet residential street within walking distance of bars and restaurants. It has spacious rooms and suites decorated with earthy tones and solid furniture. There's a pleasant garden filled with tropical foliage, breakfast included, and coffee refills all day.

$ Hostal Cumbres del Volcán
85 Av Norte 637, Col Escalón, T2207-3705, www.cumbresdelvolcan.com.
This pleasant, down-to-earth hostel in a safe neighbourhood opened its doors in 2010 and continues to receive a stream of budget travellers. Accommodation includes shared dorms and private rooms, with or without private bath and a/c. There is laundry, Wi-Fi and parking, but no kitchen.

$ Hostal Doña Marta
Pasaje Maracaibo 1-B, Urbanizacion Venezuela, T2301-3006, www.hostaldonamarta.blogspot.co.uk.
This low-key, economical, family-run hostel is safely nestled in a gated community. It's a little out of the way with few facilities in the neighbourhood, but there is a bus stop nearby. The owners are friendly and helpful and can organize airport pick-up for a fee. All rooms have shared bath.

$ Joan's Hostel
Calle del Meditarreno 12, Colonia Jardines de Guadalupe, Antiguo Cuscatlán, T7860-7157, www.joanshostal.blogspot.co.uk.
A safe, clean hostel in a quiet residential area that would suit couples or older travellers. Accommodation includes dorms and private rooms and there's a kitchen for self-catering. Note there are no signs outside so the hostel can be tricky to find. The hostess, Ana, is friendly and helpful.

Restaurants

In the older downtown area few places are open to eat after 1830. Restaurants are open later in the western sections of the city. Along Blv Hipódromo, San Benito, restaurants are generally very good, but expensive. On Blv de los Héroes there are many restaurants, including US-style fast-food places. The strip along Calle San Antonio Abad has several local eateries.

$$$ Al Pomodoro
Av La Revolución y Calle Circunvalación 184, Col San Benito, T2243-7888, www.alpomodoro.com.sv.
Nestled in the Zona Rosa next to the Sheraton hotel, this upscale and tastefully presented Italian eatery serves a variety of pastas, pizzas, seafood and meat dishes. Attentive service and they keep a good stock of wine too. Popular and reliable.

$$$ Café Café
Calle El Tanque 130, 99 Av Norte y 7 y 9 Calle Pte bis 130, T2263-4034, www.cafecafe.com.sv.
Café Café serves excellent Peruvian cuisine. Specialities include fillet of salmon with honey and orange sauce, tuna with scallop sauce, and a seafood platter with a mix of fresh prawns, octopus, and crab in a white wine sauce. Not cheap, but recommended.

$$$ El Bodegón
Paseo Escalón 3956 and 77 Av Norte, T2263-5283.
El Bodeón is a rather sober and formal San Salvador institution with very classic airs. They serve fine traditional Spanish cuisine, such as paella and *crema Catalana*. Not trendy, but romantic and dependendable.

$$$ Kamakura
93 Av Norte 617, Col Escalón T2263-2401, www.restaurantekamakura.com.
Kamakura is an authentic Japanese restaurant set inside a residential home and it serves the best sushi in town. Rolls are perfectly fresh and generously sized (try the sashimi botánico) with soups, green tea and vegetable tempura also available. Good traditional flavours; a taste of Tokyo.

$$$ La Hacienda Real
Just opposite of La Gran Vía Mall T, Km 8, Cra Panamericana, next to Air Force offices, T2243-8567, www.hacienda-real.com.
Without a doubt some of the best steaks in El Salvador, excellent service, prime beef cuts and fingerlicking food. Part of an international chain with branches in Guatemala and Honduras.

$$$ La Hola Beto's Escalón
Pasaje Dordelly 4352 between 85 and 87 Av Norte (above Paseo Escalón), www.laholabetos.com.
This long-established seafood joint has branches across the city. The ceviche and seafood soup are very good and they also serve Italian and steaks. Fresh food, great service, parking. Recommended.

$$ Automariscos
Located next to roundabout by the Don Rua church, 5a Av Norte, Blv Tutunichapa, T2226-5363, also outlet in San Benito, Av Revolución No 179 (between Pizza Hut and Anthropological museum), T2243-3653.
A family business more than 15 years in operation, Automariscos serves out-of-the-ordinary seafood and huge portions. Offerings include ceviches, soups and shrimp cocktails.

$$ El Sopón Típico
71 Av Norte and 1 Calle Pte 3702, Col Escalón, T2298-3008 and Blv de Los Héroes, Pasaje Las Palmeras 130, Urbanización Florida T2260-2671, www.elsopontipico.com.
A very relaxed and down-to-earth eatery serving typical Salvadorean soups and other dishes, including *gallo en chicha* (chicken in maize wine) and *mariscada* (seafood chowder).

$$ Kalpataru
Calle La Mascota 928 and Calle Maquilishuat, just below Arbol de Dios, www.kalpataru.com.sv. Open until 2230.
Full restaurant service and lunch buffet, good atmosphere. Best vegetarian place in town. They also offer reasonably priced yoga classes.

$$ Rustico Bistro
3a Calle Pte y Pasaje Los Pinos 3877, Col Escalón.
This place serves the best gourmet burgers in town: thick, flavourful, and cooked to taste. They also do a mean beef panini and a formidable hot dog, all with a side of Cajun-spiced fries. Awesome and highly recommended.

$$ Zócalo Escalón
71 Av Norte, T2257-6851, next to Galerías mall.
Excellent Mexican food in small, casual place, with outdoor tables; other branches around city, including Zona Rosa, San Benito and Santa Elena.

$$-$ Mercadito Merliot
Antiguo Cuscatlán.
Famous food market with fresh seafood dishes (among others).

Cafés and delís
There are numerous cafeterías serving cheap traditional meals such as *tamales*, *pupusas*, *frijoles*, rice with vegetables, etc. Often these places can be found around the major hotels.

Kreef
Plaza Kreef, 87 Av Sur and Av los Almendros Block G, Zona 11, Urbanización Maquilishuat T2264-7094, www.kreef.com.
Restaurant and deli, specialities meat and juicy chicken fillets, imported cheese, beer and wine. Live music at weekends.

La Panetière
Plaza Villaviciencio, locales 34-35, Paseo Escalón, www.lapanetiere.com.sv.
Delicious French pastry, crêpes, cappuccinos, salads, and breakfasts. Popular with foreigners, a bit pricey but worth it.

Shaw's
Paseo Escalón, 1 block west of Plaza Beethoven, Zona Rosa and at Metrocentro.
Pricey but good coffee and chocolates, also sell US magazines, a few English-language books and greetings cards.

Bars and clubs

Check for gigs in *La Prensa Gráfica* and *El Diario de Hoy*. All big hotels have their own nightclub. All discos have ladies' night on Wed and Thu when women enter free and get a discount on drinks; go in a group.

Zona Rosa, Col San Benito, has many bars/discos/open-air cafés in a well-lit area, crowded Fri-Sat nights (cover charge US$10), take bus No 30 B from near Esso/Texaco/Mundo Feliz on Blv de los Héroes before 2000, taxi thereafter. Just beyond Zona Rosa, Multiplaza and La Gran Vía malls are favourite places for going out;

both have clubs, cafés and bars where young people gather at weekends. The most popular spots in Multiplaza are **Envy**, **Stanza** and **La Cueva**.

Café La T
Opposite Centro Comercial San Luis
Run by German Anne, also has a fairtrade gift shop.

El Arpa Irlandés
Av A 137 Col San José.
Run by Gerry from Ireland.

La Luna
Calle Berlín 228, off Blvd de los Héroes, Urbanización Buenos Aires 3, T2260-2921. Wed-Sun.
Great food and atmosphere, live music some nights, decor and furniture designed by local artists. Popular and fashionable place to hang out. Reasonably priced drinks and snacks; take a taxi late at night.

Photo Café
Col El Roble, Pje 2 21, T2100-2469, near the National University.
An artsy place run by photojournalists.

Entertainment

Cinema
A few older-style cinemas in the centre are being overshadowed by the multiplexes along the Blv de los Héroes; most screenings are in English with Spanish sub-titles. Look in local press for listings. Arthouse films are shown at **La Luna** and **Café La T** (see above) for free. See schedules for events. **Alliance Française** arranges film seasons, T2223-8084.

Music, dance and theatre
Ballet and theatre at the **Teatro Nacional de Bellas Artes**, see page 24, and music or plays at the **Teatro Cámera**.

Spectator sports
Check *La Prensa Gráfica* and *El Diario de Hoy*.
Baseball On the field opposite Mercado Nacional de Artesanías, Tue-Fri 1700, Cuban and US coaches, local teams, entrance US$1.25.
Boat racing **Club Náutico** (at the Estero de Jaltepeque), is famous for its boat races across the mud flats at low tide.
Football Sun and Thu at the Cuscatlán and/or Flor Blanca stadiums.
Motor racing At the El Jabalí autodrome on lava fields near Quetzaltepeque.

Festivals

Mar/Apr Holy Week.
Jul/Aug Celebrations of **El Salvador del Mundo** are held the fortnight preceding 6 Aug. As a climax, colourful floats wend their way up the Campo de Marte (the park encompasssing Parque Infantil and Palacio de Deportes; 9 Calle Pte and Av España). On 5 Aug, an ancient image of the Saviour is borne before the large procession, before church services the next day, celebrating the **Feast of the Transfiguration**.
12 Dec Día del Indígena; there are colourful processions honouring the **Virgen de Guadalupe** (take bus No 101 to the Basílica de Guadalupe, on the Cra a Santa Tecla).

Shopping

Visa and MasterCard are accepted in most shops.

Bookshops
Magazines and newspapers in English can be bought at leading hotels and many shops sell US magazines. **Cervantes** (9 Av Sur 114 in the Centre

and Edif El Paseo 3, Paseo Escalón); **Clásicos Roxsil** (6 Av Sur 1-6, Santa Tecla, T2228-1212); **Editorial Piedra Santa** (Av Olímpica 3428, Av 65-67 Sur, T2223-5502); **Etc Ediciones** (in Centro Comercial Basilea, San Benito). Some English books at **Librería Cultural Salvadoreña** in Metrosur.

Olivos, *also café and restaurant, just below Hotel Princess, Zona Rosa, T2245-4221, www.olivoscafe.com.* Has a wide selection of books, specializing in alternative medicine and health.

Crafts

You can buy fairtrade arts and crafts at **Café La T** (see under Bars and clubs above, Calle San Antonio Abad), and **Nahanché**. Metrocentro, Centro Comercial Basilea and Multiplaza has a great selection of handicrafts from all over the country.

El Arbol de Dios, *La Mascota y Av Masferrer, T2224-6200, see page 27.* **Mercado Ex-Cuartel**, *8 Av Norte, 1 Calle Ote.* Crafts market, a few blocks east of the Teatro Nacional, rebuilt after a fire in 1995.

Mercado Nacional de Artesanías, *opposite the Estado Mayor on the road to Santa Tecla (buses 101A, B or C, 42B, 79, 34, 30B), at prices similar to the Mercado Ex-Cuartel, daily 0800-1800.* A one-stop craft shop with a good cross-section of items even if they are not that well presented. Some of the cheapest prices around.

Shopping malls

Metrocentro (large shopping mall on the Blv de los Héroes, northwest of the city centre). Together with **Metrosur** this is the largest shopping mall in Central America. Another shopping centre, **Villas Españolas** (on the Paseo Escalón, 1 block south of the Redondel Masferrer); is more exclusive, with expensive boutiques. **Galerías Escalón** (Col Escalón), has department stores and cybercafés. **El Paseo** (just at the corner of 79 Av, Escalón), is the newish mall. The area west of Zona Rosa has 3 newer malls named **Multiplaza**, **Hiper Mall Cascadas** and **La Gran Vía**.

What to do

Diving

El Salvador Divers, *Paseo Escalón 3 Calle Pte 5020, Col Escalón, T2264-0961, www.elsalvadordivers.com.* Offer weekly excursions and classes. Located behind the Villavicencio Mall.

Language schools

Centro de Intercambio y Solidaridad, Av Bolívar 103, Colonia Libertad, T2235-1330, www.cis-elsalvador.org. Spanish school in the mornings 0800-1200, English school in the afternoons 1700-1900 (volunteer English teachers needed for 10-week sessions).

Tour operators

Inter Tours, *Balam Quitze mall in Paseo Escalon, T2263-6188, www.viajero.com. sv.* One of the most recognized travel agencies in the capital. They have excellent service and can track down that special rate you need.

OTEC Turismo Joven, *Centro Comercial El Partenope, local 2, Paseo Escalón, T2264-0200.* Official ISIC office in El Salvador and STA Travel representative, offering travel assistance, reissue of lost tickets, date changes and rerouting. Special prices for students, teachers and young people with an ISIC card.

Pullmantur, *Av La Revolución, T2243-1300.* Luxury bus service to Guatemala and excellent package tours to Antigua.

Salva Natura, *33 Av Sur 640, Col Flor Blanca, T2279-1515, www.salvanatura.org*. For information about Parque Nacional El Imposible in the southwest, near Tacuba and Ataco.

Tour In El Salvador, *T2207-4155, www. tour inelsalvador.com*. Minibus tours around the country and to Guatemala and Honduras; experienced and very knowledgeable guide Jorge Martínez. Highly recommended.

Transport

Air

The international airport, Monseñor Óscar Arnulfo Romero (**SAL**), T2339-9455, www.aeropuertoelsalvador.gob. sv, at Comalapa is 62 km southeast from San Salvador towards Costa del Sol beach, reached by a 4-lane, toll highway. **Acacya** minibus to airport, from 3 Calle Pte y 19 Av Norte, T2271-4937, airport T2339-9182, at 0600, 0700, 1000, 1400 (be there 15 mins before), US$3 one-way (leaves from airport when full, on right as you go out). **Acacya** also has a taxi service, US$25, the same as other radio taxi companies; ordinary taxis charge US$20. Taxi to **La Libertad** beach US$30. To **Costa del Sol** US$50. There is a post office, a tourist office, 2 exchange desks (including Citi Bank) and duty-free shopping for both departures and arrivals.

The old airport is at Ilopango, 13 km east of the city and is primarily used by the air force and for some domestic flights.

Bus

Local Most buses stop running at 2100. City buses charge US$0.20 and microbuses charges US$0.25 within the city; make sure you have the right change or a small bill to hand. Most run 0500-2000, after which time use taxis.

Some useful routes: No 29 from Terminal de Oriente to Metrocentro via downtown; **No 30** Mercado Central to Metrocentro; **No 30B** from Mundo Feliz (100 m up from Esso station on Blv de los Héroes) to Escalón, 79 Av Norte, Zona Rosa (San Benito), Alameda Roosevelt and back to Metrocentro along 49 Av; **No 34** San Benito–Mercado de Artesanías–Terminal de Occidente–Mercado Central–Terminal Oriente; **No 52** 'Paseo' Parque Infantil– Metrocentro–Plaza Las Américas– Paseo Escalón–Plaza Masferrer; **No 52** 'Hotel' Parque Infantil– Metrocentro–Hotel Copa Airlines–Plaza Masferrer. Route **No 101** buses to/from Santa Tecla are blue and white for either class of service.

Long distance and international
Domestic services go from **Terminal de Occidente**, off Blv Venezuela, T2223-3784 (take city buses 4, 7C, 27, 44 or 34); **Terminal de Oriente**, end of Avenida Peralta in Centro Urbano Lourdes (take city buses No 29 from Metrocentro, 42 from Alameda, or No 4, from 7 C), T2281-3086, very crowded with buses and passengers, keep your eyes open for the bus you want; and **Terminal Sur**, San Marcos, Zona Franca, about 9 km from the city (take city bus No 26 from Universidad Nacional area or Avenida España downtown, take taxi to city after 1830). Terminal de Sonsonate, located just outside city centre, by main road to Acajutla T2450-4625. Terminal de Santa Ana T2440-0938. Routes and fares are given under destinations. For La Libertad and beaches west to Playa El Zonte, plenty of buses go from opposite Iglesia Ceiba Guadalupe, a short taxi ride from centre: Bus No 102 to La Libertad and

Nos 107 or 192 to Playa El Zonte, approx 1 hr, US$1.

Heading south: Recognized international bus company **Ticabus** departs from Hotel San Carlos, Calle Concepción 121, T2222-4808, www.ticabus.com. Also with an office in Blv del Hipódromo, Zona Rosa, T2243-9764. To **Tapachula** 0600 and 1200 noon, 11 hrs, US$30. To **Guatemala**, 0600 and 1300, 5 hrs, US$15. To **Tegucigalpa**, 1200, 7 hrs, US$15. To **Managua**, 0500, 12 hrs, US$30. To **San José**, 33 hrs including overnight in Managua, US$50. To **Panama City**, depart 0500, arriving 1700 next day, US$75. They now have an executive coach service to **Nicaragua** for US$44, and **Costa Rica** US$58 (both depart 0300) and to **Panama** at 0500, US$93. **King Quality**, Puerto Bus Terminal, Alameda Juan Pablo II y 19 Av Norte, T2241-8704; in Zona Rosa T2271-1361, www.king-qualityca.com. You can walk there from city centre, but it's not advisable with luggage; take bus 101D from Metrocentro, or bus 29, 52 to 21 Av Norte, 2 blocks south of terminal (city buses don't permit heavy luggage). The terminal has a *casa de cambio* (good rates) and a restaurant. They have departures to Central America and Mexico. Departure times from Puerto Bus station (check office for times from Zona Rosa).

Service to Guatemala with domestic carriers includes **Pezzarossi**, **Taca**, **Transesmer**, **Melva**, and **Vencedora**. All operate services to **Guatemala City** more or less hourly (5½ hrs, US$13). Departures between 0500 and 1600. **Confortlines** (sister company of **King Quality**) has departures to Guatemala at 0800 and 1400 for US$30 – higher-class bus than the regular service but

no meals. **Pullmantur**, T2243-1300, runs a 0700 service Mon-Sat, 0830 Sun, and a daily luxury 1500 service from Hotel Marriott Presidente in Zona Rosa for US$35, with a/c, film, drinks and meals.

Service to Mexico also from Terminal de Occidente, **El Cóndor** goes to **Talismán**, Mexico via Sonsonate, La Hachadura and Escuintla, US$12, 0330, 9½ hrs, also 0700-0800 to Guatemala City. **Transgalgos** has direct departures to Mexico from Puerto Bus.

Car

Car hire Local insurance (about US$10-15 per day plus a deductible US$1000 deposit) is mandatory and 13% IVA applies. **Avis**, 43 Av Sur 137, Colonia Flor Blanca www.avis.com.sv, T2500-2847; **Budget**, Hotel Sheraton Presidente, Col San Benito T2283-2908 and Calle Mirador and 85 Av Norte 648, Col Escalón, T2264-3888, www.budget.com; **Euro Rent-Cars**, 29 Calle Pte and 7 Av Norte 1622, T2235-5232, chamba_r@hotmail.com, cheap daily rates from US$10; **Hertz**, corner of 91 Av Nte and 9 Calle Pte, T2264-2818, www.hertz.com; **Sandoval & Co**, T2235-4405, sub-compact late-model cars from US$10 per day, English spoken.

Car repairs Modern service centres of **Record** and **Impressa**, are found throughout the capital. Good source of spare parts found at **Super Repuestos**, T2221-4440.

Insurance **Asesuiza** is widely used for car insurance, T2209-5025, as is **La Centroamericana**, T2298-6666.

Car papers **Ministerio de Hacienda**, T2226-1900, 'Tres Torres', turn left on Blv de los Héroes, 300 m past Texaco station.

Taxi

Plenty (all yellow), don't have meters, ask fare before getting in. Trips within San Salvador will have a mininum cost of US$4 and most trips will be between US$4 and US$7. Airport is approximately US$25. Few drivers speak English. They will charge more in the rain. More expensive radio taxis may be hired through **Acacya**, T2271-4937.

Western
El Salvador

West of San Salvador, lush green hills and rolling cattle pastures are punctuated by indigenous and colonial villages on the approach to Sonosante, an important agricultural centre basking in volcanic shadows.

Beyond it, the Ruta de las Flores is one of El Salvador's prime attractions. Disarming cobblestone streets, colonial airs, craft traditions, culinary highlights, vibrant festivals and a thriving art scene make the communities on this 40-km-long route a popular weekend getaway. Steeped in tranquil coffee fincas and arresting mountain views, the surrounding countryside is ideal for hiking and horse riding too.

North of the Ruta de las Flores, little indigenous villages and pre-Columbian ruins contrast with the vibrancy of Santa Ana, El Salvador's second largest city. The big attractions here are Lago de Coatepeque and the wilderness of Parque Nacional Cerro Verde, home to the peak of Volcán Santa Ana. Three routes lead to Guatemala, the northernmost passing close to Metapán and the impressive cloudforests of Parque Nacional Montecristo on the border with Honduras.

gateway to the Ruta de las Flores

From the junction with the Pan-American Highway, just west of Colón, route CA 8 heads west, past Armenia, to the town of Izalco (population 70,959) at the foot of Izalco volcano (8 km from Sonsonate, bus 53C). The town has evolved from the gradual merging of the *ladino* village of Dolores Izalco and the indigenous village of Asunción Izalco. In colonial times this was an important trading centre and in 1932 it experienced a communist rebellion. Today the town is enjoying a tourist revival thanks to its colonial architecture, its prominent and active indigenous population, and its rich heritage of religious imagery which blends indigenous and Roman Catholic beliefs.

A week-long festival celebrating El Salvador del Mundo runs 8-15 August and there is also a local celebration from 24 November to 10 December. The Feast of John the Baptist runs from 17-24 June.

Sonsonate

Sonsonate (altitude 225 m, population 71,541), 64 km from the capital, is the country's chief cattle-raising region. It also produces sugar, tobacco, rice, tropical fruits, hides and balsam. The city was founded in 1552 and is hot, dirty and crowded, but worth checking out for its colonial architecture in the city centre. The beautiful **El Pilar** church (1723) is strongly reminiscent of the church of El Pilar in San Vicente. The **cathedral** has many cupolas (the largest covered with white porcelain) and was badly damaged in the 2001 earthquake but is now fully restored. The old church of **San Antonio del Monte** (completed 1861), 1 km from the city, draws pilgrims from afar (fiesta 22-26 August). There is a small **railway museum**, look for the locomotive at the entrance to the city on the highway from San Salvador (Km 65). An important market is held each Sunday. In the northern outskirts of the city there is a waterfall on the Río Sensunapán. Legend has it that an indigenous princess drowned there, and on the anniversary of her death a gold casket appears below the falls.

> **Tip...**
> The town of Izalco and Izalco volcano are not directly connected by road. A paved road branches off the Pan-American Highway 14 km before the turning for Izalco town and goes up towards Volcán Izalco.

The main annual event is **Feria de la Candelaria** in February. Easter Week processions are celebrated with particular fervour and are probably the most impressive in the whole country. On Easter Thursday and Holy Friday the streets are filled with thousands of members of the *cofradías* (brotherhoods).

Around Sonsonate

There are several **waterfalls** and other sites of natural beauty in the Sonsonate district. To the west, near the village of **Santo Domingo de Guzmán** (bus No 246 from Sonsonate), are the falls of **El Escuco** (2 km north), **Tepechapa**

(1.5 km further) and **La Quebrada** (further still up the Río Tepechapa), all within walking distance of both Santo Domingo and each other. Walk through the town then follow the river; there are several spots to swim. Santo Domingo de Guzmán is also known for its *alfarería* (pottery) of *comales*, clay plates used to create tortillas and *pupusas* over the open fire, and its many Náhuatl-speaking habitants. There's a festival in Santo Domingo, 24-25 December.

A short distance north is **San Pedro Puxtla** (bus No 246), with a modern church built on the remains of an 18th-century edifice. From here you can visit the **Tequendama Falls** on the Río Sihuapán. Bus No 219 goes east to **Cuisnahuat** (with an 18th-century baroque church), where the Fiesta de San Judas takes place 23-29 November. From there it is 2 km south to the Río Apancoyo, or 4 km north to **Peñón El Escalón** (covered in balsam trees) and **El Istucal Cave**, at the foot of the Escalón hill, where indigenous rites are celebrated in November.

Listings Izalco to Sonsonate

Where to stay

Izalco

$$ La Casona de Los Vega
2a Av Norte 24, in the centre. T2453-5951, www.lacasonadelosvega.com.sv.
An atmospheric colonial home converted into a comfortable hotel and restaurant. Pleasant garden and good views. Tours available.

$ El Chele
Final Av Roberto Carillas, Calle La Violeta, Caserío Texcalito, T2453-6740. Ricardo Salazar, T7798-8079.
Located some 800 m north of Izalco at a finca surrounded by forest, this place has a great view of Volcán Izalco. Escorted hikes and horse rides available to Cerro Verde and its surrounding slopes and Izalco with visits to 2 pre-Columbian ruins nearby. Free transport available, call to arrange. English spoken.

Sonsonate

$$ Agape
Km 63 on outskirts of town, take old road through Sonsonate, the hotel is on the
exit street to San Salvador, just before the main roundabout on the right side, T2451-2667, www.hotelagape.com.sv.
Adequate suites and rooms with a/c or fan, safe parking, restaurant, gardens, cable TV, pool and laundry service.

Restaurants

Izalco
There are several *comedores* in town.

$$ Casa de Campo
Across from Turicentro Atecozol, T2453-6530. Open weekends only.
The old *casco* of the finca **Cuyancúa** has been restored with beautiful gardens, making it a good spot for a meal. The fish raised in the artificial lake is served in the restaurant. Horses are available for hire.

$ Mariona
In the centre, T2453-6580.
This *comedor* serves a 55-year-old recipe for *sopa de gallina* (Creole chicken soup) which is famous all over Izalco.

$ Restaurante El Cheles
In the centre of Izalco with another branch out of town at Final Av Roberto Carillas, Calle La Violeta, Caserío Texcalito, T2453-5392.
Owner Ricardo Salazar speaks English and can arrange escorted hikes and horse riding to Cerro Verde.

Sonsonate

$$ Doña Laura
Inside Hotel Agape (see Where to stay, above). Open 0730-2100.
Highly recommended.

Transport

Sonsonate
Bus No 248 to **Santa Ana**, US$1.50 along Carr 12 north, 39 km, a beautiful journey. To **Ahuachapán**, bus No 249, 2 hrs, slow, best to go early in the day. To Ataco, via Juayúa and Ahuachapán, No 23, US$1, 1½ hrs To **Barra de Santiago**, bus No 285. To **Los Cobanos** bus No 259. Take care at the bus terminal and on rural routes (eg in Nahuizalco area). From **San Salvador** to Sonsonate by bus No 530, US$0.80, 1½ hrs, very frequent.

Ruta de las Flores

flower-festooned villages filled with culture and tradition

★Steeped in fragrant coffee groves and bucolic highland scenery, El Salvador's legendary Ruta de las Flores climbs northwest towards Ahuachapán, gently wending on Route CA 8.

Driving at leisure is the best way to explore the region, but frequent buses from Sonsonate (bus 249 and 285, two hours) also cover the 40-km stretch. It is also possible to access the Ruta de las Flores from Santa Ana in the opposite direction.

Nahuizalco
The route begins just beyond the indigenous village of Nahuizalco (population 49,081). Some of the older women here still wear the *refajo* (a doubled length of cloth made of tie-dyed threads worn over a wrap-round skirt), and various crafts are still made, including wood and rattan furniture. Although use of the indigenous language is dying out, you do still encounter people who speak Náhuatl. The night market, unique in El Salvador, opens at dusk and has traditional local food on sale. There's a religious festival 19-25 June, with music, **Danza de los Historiantes** and art exhibitions; also 24-25 December, with music and **Danza de los Pastores**. Take bus 53 D from Sonsonate.

Salcoatitán and Juayúa
Further up the mountainside at Km 82 is **Salcoatitán** (population 5484) at 1045 m above sea level, a colonial village with a beautiful park in front of the colonial church. This cosy village used to be only a drive-through on the way to Juayúa or Apaneca but has experienced a tourist revival lately with several new restaurants, art galleries and artisan shops.

Further along, the road branches off to Juayúa 2 km further north and the same bus from Sonsonate takes a detour into the village and back. **Juayúa** is the largest city on the Ruta de Las Flores – the name means 'River of Purple Orchids' in the local Náhuatl dialect – and sits nestled in a valley dominated by volcanoes. It's a peaceful spot where you can watch people at work and kids playing in the semi-cobbled street. The surrounding region is blanketed in coffee groves; the bean was introduced to the area in 1838 and today the town produces about 10% of the coffee exported from El Salvador. Its church houses an image of the **Cristo Negro** (Black Christ) carved by Quirio Cataño at the end of the 16th century. **Tourist information** is available from Jaime Salgado, at **Juayutur** ① *T2469-2310, juayutur@navegante. com.sv.* He can provide good information about the activities available in the region, which include rappelling waterfalls, the hike of the seven waterfalls and the mountain lagoon with wild horses. Guides are trained local youngsters. Also check out the **Casa de la Cultura**, on the corner next to the park for information on Juayúa. Gaby and Julio Vega, the owners of **Akwaterra Tours** ① *www.aventuraelsalvador. com,* run a mountain cabin at Finca Portezuelo named **La Escondida**; also a camping site with ready made-up tents on decks under covers. They're fluent in English and offer a wide range of activites at **Portezuelo Adventure Park** such as hiking, mountain biking, horseback riding, zip-wire circuit, ATVs and paragliding.

There are a number of excursions you can do in the area to see wildlife, including river otters, toucans, butterflies and many other animals. In the dry season **Laguna de las Ranas** (Laguna Seca) dries up, attracting numerous reptiles as it shrinks. There are also trips to the 30-m-high waterfall at **Salto el Talquezal**, the 50-m-high **Salto de la Lagunilla Azul** and several other waterfalls in the region (seven in one day if you take a tour), with swimming and picnics on the way (see below). Every weekend Juayúa celebrates the Feria Gastronómica, an opportunity to try a variety of traditional dishes, often accompanied by local events, music and shows.

The **Feria Gastrónomica Internacional** is in January and celebrates with dishes from all over the world; other festivals include Día de los Canchules (31 October), when people ask for candies and **Día de las Mercedes** (17 September), when the houses are decorated with branches and candles leading up to the procession of the Virgen de la Merced. Another local attraction is the **Museo del Café**, of the coffee cooperative **La Majada** ① *T2467-9008 ext 1451, www.cafemajadaoro.com. sv,* located in **San José La Majada**, just outside Juayua on the road to Los Naranjos. Tours include information on coffee processing and a trip to the processing plant. A coffee shop offers local brews and iced coffee.

Apaneca

Between Ahuachapán and Sonsonate, 91 km from San Salvador and 29 km from Las Chinamas on the border, is Apaneca (altitude 1450 m, population 8383), an extremely peaceful town (and the highest town in the country), with small cobbled streets, marking the summit of the **Ruta de las Flores**. Founded by Pedro de Alvarado in 1543, Apaneca is known for its cool climate and winds – *apaneca* means 'rivers of wind' in Náhuatl.

The town has a colonial centre, a traditional *parque* and a municipal market selling fruit, flowers and handicrafts. One of the oldest parochial churches in the country used to corner the central park but was demolished after damage caused by the 2001 earthquake. It has been partially reconstructed, with a modern twist. The artisan market is a great place to see the local arts and crafts. Other local industries include coffee, flowers for export and furniture. Have a look at the topiary creations outside the police station and check out the **Casa de la Cultura** in the centre of town.

There are two small lakes nearby to the north, **Laguna Verde** and **Laguna Las Ninfas**, whose crater-like walls are clothed in tropical forest and cypress trees. It is possible to swim in the former, but the latter is too shallow and reedy. According to local legend, a swim is meant to be very beneficial to your health and the lakes are very popular with tourists. This is the Cordillera de Apaneca, part of the narrow highland belt running southeast of Ahuachapán.

South of Apaneca is the **Cascada del Río Cauta**. To get there, take bus No 216 from Ahuachapán towards Jujutla, alight 3 km after the turn-off to Apaneca, then walk 300 m along the trail to the waterfall.

In the grounds of Finca Santa Leticia lies an **archaeological site** ⓘ *US$2; 2-hr coffee tour US$20; both combined US$35, www.hotelsantaleticia.com, bus No 249 from Juayúa (10 mins)*. It is believed to be 2600 years old and was rediscovered in 1968 by the farm owner. Three huge monuments are buried among the coffee groves and you feel like a first-time discoverer as you travel the winding route to get there. There are three stone spheres with human characteristics weighing between 6000 and 11,000 kg.

Ataco

Concepción de Ataco, to give the town its full name, located just below Apaneca, is now a favourite on the Ruta de Las Flores. The village has undergone a complete renovation, and now has cobbled streets, old-fashioned benches and streetlights, and a popular weekend festival with food, flowers, and arts and crafts. Some excellent coffee shops and restaurants, offering cuisine from Mexico to France, continue to open up, mainly for weekends only, making Ataco one of the most visited villages in the area, and well worth a weekend trip.

Look for the *marimba* and the traditional dances in the main square and drop by **Diconte & Axul**, an artsy café that offers anything from delicious home-made pies to original arts and crafts that are giving La Palma art a run for their money. The **House of Coffee** has an espresso machine and serves the excellent world-class coffee grown in Ataco at their own finca for five generations.

Ahuachapán

Coffee is the main export of Ahuachapán (altitude 785 m, population 110,511), a quiet town with low and simple houses. One of the most popular local sights is the geothermal field of **Los Ausoles**, 3 km road from Ahuachapan and marked on the road out of town to Apaneca as 'Planta Geotérmica'. You can't go into the plant, but when you arrive take the road to the right where, just a little way up the hill on the left, you come to a little house, geysers of boiling mud with plumes of steam and strong whiffs of sulphur. The *ausoles* are used for generating 30% of the country's electricity. For a small tip the house owner will take you into his back garden to see the fumaroles and boiling pools.

Taking the northern road from Ahuachapán, 9 km west of town near the village of **Los Toles** are the **Tehuasilla Falls**, where the Río El Molino falls 60 m (take bus No 293 from Ahuachapán to Los Toles, then walk 1 km). The road continues northwest through the treeless **Llano del Espino**, with its small lake, and across the Río Paz into Guatemala.

Around Ahuachapán

Tacuba (population 29,585) is an indigenous town, around 850 m above sea level, and 15 km west of Ahuachapán. Tacuba means 'the village of the football game', probably relating to the *juego de pelota* of the Maya, and the existence of many pre-Columbian mounds in the surrounding area suggest the region was heavily populated in the past. At the entrance to the town are the largest colonial church ruins in El Salvador, torn down by the earthquake of Santa Marta, the same tremors that ruined large parts of Antigua, Guatemala, in 1773. You can also visit the Casa de la Cultura office, **Concultura** ⓘ *3 km on main st north, daily 0900-1230 and 1330-1600*, to see an interesting display of photos. The town is near the northern entrance of Parque Nacional El Imposible (see page 65), which is accessed by hiking or 4WD in the dry season.

The surrounding area offers a wide range of opportunities including waterfalls, pristine rivers, mountain hikes and panoramic views. **Ceiba de los Pericos**, 15 minutes out of Tacuba by car, is a 600-year-old ceiba tree where thousands of parrots flock together at dusk to sleep in its branches, ending the day with a deafening noise before resting for the night. In Tacuba centre the **Ceiba de las Garzas** is the rendezvous of hundreds of *garzas* (herons).

Local tour company **El Imposible Tours**, led by Tacuba native Manolo González, provide tours of the Tacuba area and to Parque Nacional El Imposible (see page 50). The dirt road leading from Tacuba to the cordillera is steep and spectacular and provides impressive views; it is recommended although a 4WD is required.

Where to stay

Salcoatitán and Juayúa
Check www.juayua.com for a complete list of hotels and restaurants in this area.

$$$-$ La Escondida
*6 km north of Juayúa at Finca
El Portezuelo, T7888-4552,
www.akwa terra.com.*
B&B in an exceptionally beautiful location, in a coffee plantation cradled between Laguna Verde and forest-clad mountains, with a view over to Ahuachapán to the north. Cosily furnished rooms, with fireplace, DVD, equipped kitchen. Contact Julio and Gaby (English spoken). They also offer coffee decks – a tent protected by a roofed wooden structure – and camping.

$$ Hotel Juayúa
*Urb Esmeralda, Final 6a Av Norte, Juayúa,
T2469-2109, www.hoteljuayua.net.*
A rustic and intimate little guesthouse with fine views from the garden and a pool. Rooms are cosy, tranquil and comfortable. Rates include breakfast and internet.

$$-$ El Mirador
*A block from the park, Juayúa, T2452-2432, www.hotelelmiradorjuayua.
blogspot.co.uk.*
A 3-storey building with restaurant on top. Rooms include cable TV, fan, private bath with hot water. There is a cheap backpackers' dorm too. Best option for low rates and central location.

$ Anahuac
*1 Calle Pte and 5 Av Norte, Juayúa,
T2469-2401, www.hotelanahuac.com.*
Dorms and private rooms for backpackers and tours, with garden, hammocks and a book exchange. The very friendly owner Cesar also runs nearby **Café Cadejo** (live music at weekends); extremely popular and highly recommended.

$ Doña Mercedes
*29 Av Sur, 6 Calle Oriente 3-6, Juayúa,
1 block south of Farmacia Don Bosco,
T2452-2287.*
Spotless accommodation and very attentive, grandmotherly service. Discounts for longer stays. A welcoming family. Recommended.

$ Hostal Casa Mazeta
*4 blocks from main square opposite
the church, Juayúa, T2406-3403,
www.casamazeta.com.*
Great backpackers' hostel in former family home, cosy rooms, dorm and covered hammock space, with garden, kitchen, Wi-Fi and lounge area with DVD library. French owner, also speaks English, German and Spanish. Tours, parking space and laundry. Recommended.

Apaneca

$$$ Santa Leticia
*Cra Sonsonate Km 86.5, south
of Apaneca, T2433-0357,
www.hotelsantaleticia.com.*
Nestled inside the Santa Leticia coffee finca, this mountain resort features comfortable double rooms decorated in locally carved wood, a solar-heated pool, gardens, and tranquil highland views. There is also a restaurant with live music on Sun. Offers access to Santa Leticia archaeological site.

$$ Las Cabañas de Apaneca
T2433-0500, Cra Sonsonate Km 90, south of Apaneca, www.cabanasapaneca.com.
Las Cabañas de Apaneca offers 17 simple but comfortable rooms set in a well-tended garden with views. Each has their own terrace with seats, hot water and cable TV. More expensive with full board.

$$-$ Hostal Rural las Orquídeas
Av Central Sur 4, T2433-0061.
This centrally located option promises clean, simple rooms and accessible prices. Also offer accommodation in a family home.

Laguna Verde

$$ Hotel Laguna Verde Guest House
T7859-2865.
A nice small house and a wood cabin located at the rim of a deep secondary crater with a spectacular view. Located 250 m from Laguna Verde and 3 km from Apaneca, a perfect departure point for hiking in the area. Microbuses serve the area several times a day; check current schedules.

Ataco

$$$ Alicante Montaña
Cra Sonsonate Km 93.5, between Apaneca and Ataco, T2433-0175, www.alicanteapaneca.com.
26 very clean log cabin rooms with hot water, cable TV. Huge, barn-like restaurant, attentive service and good value meals, pool, spa and jacuzzi; attractive grounds with aviary. Very friendly and helpful. Recommended.

$$$ Casa Degraciela
1a Calle Ote y 2a Av Nte 2, Barrio El Centro, T7546-7124, www.casadegraciela.com.
A beautiful boutique option set in an authentic, historical, colonial-style building complete with a sumptuous garden. Rooms are handsomely attired with antique furnishings and earthy tones. The building has been in the family for 150 years. Recommended.

$$$ El Carmen Estate
Km 97 Cra Sonsonate, on the edge of town, T2243-0304, www.elcarmenestate.com.
The Carmen Coffee estate has 2 types of accommodation, both very tasteful and intriguing lodgings. The Casona is the original plantation house, over 100 years old but renovated for modern use, while the Quinta is a country villa, suitable for a family or group (it's also possible to rent single rooms here). Recommended.

$$$ Hotel Mision de Angeles
Final 4a Av Norte, on the edge of town on a hill, T2404-1800, www.misiondeangeles.com.
The 10 boutique rooms at the Mision de Angéles are stylish and simple. They feature solid wood furniture, tasteful local artwork, muted tones and wood beams; some have balconies with mountain views. Great restaurant overlooking the countryside.

$$$-$$ Los Portones de Ataco
2a Av Sur 2, T6114-8030, www. losportonesdeataco.webstudio503.com.
Los Portones is a new *hostal*. It offers comfortable, simple, homely rooms with cable TV, hot water and internet. The on-site café serves good food and local coffee. Rates negotiable.

$$ El Jardín de Celeste

Cra Sononate Km 94, between Apaneca and Ataco, T2433-0277, www.eljardinde celeste.com.

10 rustic cabins with local flair located in a coffee grove and surrounded by colourful plants. The restaurant has capacity for larger parties and conventions. Beautifully decorated throughout the place with antiques, orchids, plants and arts and crafts.

$$ La Posada de Don Oli

1a Av Sur, entre 2 and 4 Calle Pte, T2450-5155, oogomezduarte@yahoo.com.mx.

Hotel and restaurant in a colonial setting, owned by the local mayor, Oscar Gómez. Guides available for visits to the local sights. Simple, no-frills, family-run digs.

Ahuachapán

$$$-$$ Termales de Santa Teresa

Beneficio Bendix, Cra hacia Ataco, frente a Ciudadela, southeast of Ahuachapán (see website for directions), T7696-4647, www.termalesdesantateresa.com.

Mineral-rich hot springs, channelled into various bathing pools, are the unique selling point of this affordable resort. Lodgings consist of 4 bungalows, all well-attired. The best is 'Emabajada de Japón', complete with its own private pool and tasteful, traditional furnishings. Great low-season and mid-week discounts.

$$ Casa Blanca

2 Av Norte y Calle Gerardo Barrios, T2443-1505.

A simple, no-frills and charming little hotel with spotless rooms overlooking a courtyard. Good central location, breakfast included. Recommended.

$$-$ La Casa de Mamapán

Pasaje La Concordia, T2413-2507, www. lacasademamapan.com.

Nestled in the Centro Histórico near the church, Casa de Mamapán is a comfortable, colonial-style, well-renovated historic building and family-run choice with 10 rooms, all equipped with a/c, fan, Wi-Fi, hot water and cable TV. Don't miss the colourful mural on the outside wall, the work of 2 local brothers.

Around Ahuachapán

$$ La Cabaña de Tacuba

Tacuba, 50 m west of Alcaldía, T2417-4332.

Nice hotel with large park grounds, access to river and swimming pools, a/c, cable TV. Great food at the restaurant.

$ Hostal de Mama y Papa

Tacuba, Barrio El Calvario, 1 Calle 1, T2417-4268, www.imposibletours.com.

Home of the delightful González family, dorm and private rooms with private bath available; roof terrace, DVDs, Wi-Fi access, crazy ducks guard the garden. Excellent, cheap food. The son, Manolo, runs El Imposible Tours, one of the most adventurous and expert outfits in the country; see What to do, page 50.

Restaurants

Salcoatitán and Juayúa

Each weekend the whole central plaza of Juayua is invaded by the Gastronomical Food Fair; grab a chair and a table if you can, the event attracts folks from far and near. During the week there are several other options.

$$ El Cadejo Café

Calle Monseñor Romero.

This excellent bohemian café-bar has a pleasant outdoor patio and hosts occasional live music. They serve great pub grub and snacks, including wholesome sandwiches, as well as beer and iced coffee. Good vibe, especially after dark.

$$ Restaurante R&R
Calle Merceditas Careres 1-2, T2452-2083.
The best restaurant in town serves excellent grilled chicken and meat, including steak rubbed in coffee. There are also vegetarian options. Filling and flavourful comfort food from a Salvadorean chef trained in Canada. Recommended.

$ Comedor Laura's
1 block from the park on 1 Av Sur, Juayúa, T2452-2098. Daily 0700-2000.
'The best in town' according to one reader, serving *comida a la vista.*

$ Parque Restaurante La Colina
Km 82 on the turn-off between Juayúa and Salcoatitán, T2452-2916.
Old timer in the region, popular with families, also has hammocks for relaxation after the meal as well as cabins and horse rides for the kids.

$ Taquería La Guadalupana
Av Daniel Cordón Sur and 2a Calle Ote, Juayúa T2452-2195.
Authentic Mexican grub including hearty tacos. Popular with the local youth.

Cafés

Pastelería y Cafetería Festival
4 Calle Pte and 1 Av Sur, T2452-2269.
Bakery and coffee shop – try the *pastelitos de ciruela* (plum pie) or the traditional *semita*. Good view overlooking the park.

Apaneca
Stalls in the municipal market offer cheap meals and typical dishes. Try the *budín* at the middle stall on the right side of market entrance (might be the best in El Salvador). A definite must for those on a budget or for experiencing local food.

$$$-$$ La Cocina de Mi Abuela
2 Calle Pte y 1 Av Sur 5, T2433-0100. Weekends; and Cabañas de Apaneca.
The 2 largest restaurants, and the most popular spots. Attract people from far and wide.

$$ El Rosario
By the turn-off at Km 95 Cra Sonsonate, between Apaneca and Ataco, T2433-0205.
Offers different grilled dishes, from regular *churrascos* to *pelibuey* (a mix between goat and sheep), *jaripeo* (Salvadorean version of rodeo), horse shows and musical entertainments weekends.

$$ Entre Nubes
Km 93.5 Cra Sonsonate, T2433-0345, www.entrenubescafe.com.
Exceptionally beautiful nursery plants surround this fine coffee shop (open weekends) and open-air restaurant. They serve *comida típica* in addition to great desserts and varieties of coffee.

$$ Parque Ecoturístico Las Cascadas de Don Juan
T2273-1380, lascascadasdedonjuan@yahoo.com.
Serving typical dishes and also offer hikes to the waterfalls, freshwater springs as well as a camping area.

$ Laguna Verde Restaurant
Km 3.5 Carr El Caserío by La Laguna Verde, T2261-0167. Only open weekends.
A cosy and rustic spot serving typical dishes of the region.

Ataco

$$-$ The House of Coffee
T2450-5353, thoc@hotmail.com. Tue-Sun.
A must visit, the café has the only
professional espresso machine in town.
Home-made cakes and steaming hot
'Cup of Excellence' award-winning
coffee is available here.

$$-$ Tayua
T7233-6508.
A gem of a place 2 blocks uphill from
the plaza, run by English-speaking and
trained chef Veronica, and her husband.
Wide range of dishes usually using
home-produced organic veg from the
restaurant's own garden. Antique decor
and background jazz. They also have a
bakery, producing the best bread and
pastries in town.

Ahuachapán
There are a handful of restaurants with
lake views by Laguna del Espino just
outside Ahuachapán.

**$$ Restaurant El Paseo, Restaurant
Tanya and El Parador**
On the Las Chinamas road.
All serve good meals.

What to do

Apaneca
Tour operators
Apaneca Aventura, *Calle Los Platanares
2, T2433-0470, apanecaaventura@yahoo.
com.* Specialize in off-road buggy rides
around the mountains and forests,
including to Laguna Verde and Ausole
de Santa Teresa geysers and thermal
baths. English manager Becky, and

with English-speaking guides. Highly
recommended.

Tacuba
El Imposible Tours, *see Hostal de
Mama y Papa, page 48.* Range of
activities including mountain biking,
canyoning and hiking; overnight trips
combining tour of Barra de Santiago and
mangroves. Highly recommended.

Transport

Apaneca
Bus Local buses stop by the plaza,
others pass on the main road, a few
blocks north, leaving you with a fairly
long walk. Laguna Verde can be reached
on foot from Apaneca to Cantón Palo
Verde and Hoyo de Cuajuste, then a
further 1 km from where the road ends.

Ahuachapán
Bus Ahuachapán is 100 km from **San
Salvador** by bus 202, US$0.90, every
20 mins, 0430-1830 to the capital, 2 hrs
via Santa Ana. Microbuses to **border**
from northwest corner of the Parque,
US$0.45, 25 mins, slower buses same
price; see also Border crossing box for
El Salvador– Guatemala, page 111. Bus
No 210 to **Santa Ana** 1 hr, US$0.50. Bus
No 235 El Express to **Metapán** 1¼ hrs,
US$0.90. Frequent buses and minivans to
the border at Km 117.

Tacuba
Bus Buses leave the terminal in
Ahuachapán every 30 mins, 0500-1530,
return 1630-1700, via **Ataco**; US$0.60,
45 mins, rough road.

The new Pan-American Highway parallels the old one, continuing northwest to the border with Guatemala at San Cristóbal. Santa Ana, acting as a transport hub, has routes out to Ahuachapán to the west and the border at Las Chinamas, as well as north to Metapán and beyond to the border crossing of Anguiatú. See box, page 111.

Fifteen kilometres from Santa Tecla, 7 km beyond the junction with the Sonsonate road, there is a junction to the right. This road forks immediately, right to **Quezaltepeque**, left (at Joya de Cerén café) to **San Juan Opico**. After a few kilometres on the San Juan road, you cross the railway by the Kimberley-Clark factory.

★Joya de Cerén
T2401-5782, www.fundar.org.sv/joyadeceren, Tue-Sun 0900-1600, US$3, parking US$1. See Transport, page 54.

After the girder bridge crossing the Río Sucio there is a grain store beside which is Joya de Cerén (32 km from the capital). This is a major archaeological site and on the World Heritage List of UNESCO (the only one in El Salvador), not for spectacular temples, but because this is the only known site where ordinary Maya houses have been preserved having been buried by the ash from the nearby Laguna Caldera volcano in about AD 600. Buildings and construction methods can be clearly seen; a painted book and household objects have been found. All the structures are covered with protective roofing. The site has a small but good museum, café, toilets and car park. Official tours are in Spanish but English-language tours are available upon request.

San Andrés
Tue-Sun 0900-1600, US$3, popular for weekend picnics, otherwise it's quiet. Has a café. Take bus No 201 from Terminal de Occidente, US$1.50 (same bus from Santa Ana) T2319-3220, www.fundar.org.sv/sanandre.

Back on the main road, heading west is the excavated archaeological site of San Andrés, halfway between Santa Tecla and Coatepeque on the estate of the same name (its full name is La Campana de San Andrés). It is located at Km 32.5 on the Pan-American Highway, just after the Hilasal towel factory. A **museum** at the site displays some of the ceramics found (others can be seen at the Museo Nacional de Antropología David J Guzmán – MUNA – in San Salvador, see page 26). The museum also features a special indigo section with information about this natural dye. El Salvador was the number one producer of indigo in the world during the colonial era. A large indigo *obraje* (processing basin) – probably the largest found in Latin America – was found at San Andrés during an archaeological excavation and has been preserved. There are good views of the nearby hills.

Lago de Coatepeque

At El Congo, 13 km before Santa Ana, a branch road leads south to the northern shore of the beautiful Lago de Coatepeque, a favourite weekend resort, with good sailing, watersports and fishing, near the foot of Santa Ana Volcano. Many weekend homes line the north and east shores, making access to the water difficult, but there are public *balnearios*. The lakeside hotels are a good option for having a meal and to use their infrastructure for the day. You can also get boat rides on the lake through the hotels or by independent fishermen. There are *aguas termales* (hot springs) on the opposite side of the lake. A ride is between US$15 and US$45. There are two islands in the lake – **Anteojos** which is close to the hotels, and **Teopán** on the far side. The local Fiesta del Santo Niño de Atocha runs from 25-29 June.

Cerro Verde, Volcán Izalco and Volcán Santa Ana

Park entrance US$1, passport or photocopy required, car park US$0.70. Guided tour to the summit of Izalco or Santa Ana is included, leaving from the entrance daily 1100. The guided tour through the nature trail around the Cerro Verde Summit is US$0.25 per person and is led by local trained guides. The Turicentro Cerro Verde (the summit of Cerro Verde with its trails, the car park and departure point for the hikes to the volcano) is run by the Ministry of Tourism, for information T2222-8000, www. elsalvador.travel. The whole area covering the volcanoes Santa Ana, Cerro Verde and Izalco and surrounding area are part of the Parque Nacional de los Volcanes, which is administrated by Salvanatura, T2279-1515, www.salvanatura.org. To access Cerro Verde, take bus No 208 from Santa Ana at 0800, passing El Congo at 0815 to catch the 1100 departure. If you come from Sonsonate side, take the No 209 bus from Sonsonate to Cerro Verde.

From El Congo a road runs south, around the east shore of Lago Coatepeque. This road is locally known as Carretera Panorámica, due to the fantastic view of Coatepeque on one side and the mountains and valleys beyond the ridge. After reaching the summit, the paved road branches right, climbing above the south end of the lake to ★**Parque Nacional Cerro Verde** (2030 m) with its fine and surprising views of the Izalco volcano (1910 m), and Santa Ana volcano (2381 m), the highest volcano in the country. In October 2005, Santa Ana erupted for the first time in more than 100 years. The road up to Cerro Verde is lined with beautiful flowers and halfway up there is a mirador with a great view of Lago Coatepeque. Cerro Verde is probably one of the most beautiful places in El Salvador due to the special flora and fauna, breathtaking views and fine volcano trekking.

> **Tip...**
> For the best view of Izalco, go in the morning, although the afternoon clouds around the cone can be enchanting.

A 30-minute walk along a nature trail leads you around the crater ridge, to a series of miradors with views of Lago Coatepeque and Santa Ana volcano. For information on climbing Volcán Izalco, see box, opposite.

The old hotel and its volcano-view terrace were destroyed in the 2001 earthquake but you can still go there for an amazing view over Izalco volcanic

ON THE ROAD

Climbing Izalco

Izalco, as can be seen from the lack of vegetation, is a geologically young volcano. Historical records show that activity began in the 17th century as a sulphurous smoke vent but, in February 1770, violent eruptions formed a cone that was more or less in constant activity until 1957. There was a small eruption in 1966 through a blowhole on the southeast slope testified by two 1000-m lava flows. Since that time, it has been quiescent.

A path leads off the road (signposted) just below the car park on Cerro Verde. In 20-30 minutes, descend to the saddle between Cerro Verde and Izalco, then it's one to 1½ hours up (steep but manageable). The contrast between the green forest of Cerro Verde and the coal-black lava around Izalco is impressive. The climb is three hours from base. Beware of falling rocks when climbing. There's a spectacular view from the top so try to ensure that low cloud is not expected before planning to go. For a quick descent, find a rivulet of soft volcanic sand and half-slide, half-walk down in 15 minutes, then it's about one hour back up the saddle. This 'cinder running' requires care, strong shoes and consideration for those below.

If you wish to climb the volcano you need to take the first bus to Cerro Verde, as the park rangers wait for the passengers from this bus before they start the guided climb to the volcano at 1100.

crater. There are now a couple of cabins available for US$35-55. For information call the **Turicentro** ⓘ *T7949-2751.*

Where to stay

Lago de Coatepeque

$ Amacuilco
300 m from Telecom, T7822-4061.
Undergoing renovation at time of writing but still open, this place has 6 basic but clean and airy rooms, some with lake view, and hammocks. Discounts for longer stays, *marimba* classes, Spanish and Náhuatl lessons, and an art gallery. All meals available, pool, great view with jetty over the lake, secure, boat excursions on lake, tours arranged from US$30-40 per day, kayaks and bikes for rent. Run by a very helpful manager called Sandra. Recommended.

Restaurants

Lago de Coatepeque

$$$-$$ Rancho Alegre
Eastern shore of the lake near Santa Catarina church, T2441-6071, www. restauranteranchoalegresv.com.
The Rancho's offerings include a variety of *comida típica* with meat fare, such as grilled steak or rabbit in tomato sauce; soups; chicken; and seafood,

including breaded shrimps or fillet. A great setting on the lake and they offer accommodation too (**$$**).

Transport

Joya de Cerén
Bus No 108 from **San Salvador** Terminal de Occidente to San Juan; US$0.45, 1 hr. Bus No 201 from **Santa Ana**, US$0.60, 1 hr, ask the bus driver to drop you at Desvío Opico from where you can catch another bus to Joya de Cerén.

Lago de Coatepeque
Bus From **Santa Ana**, bus No 220 'El Lago' to the lake every 30 mins, US$0.35. From **San Salvador**; bus No 201 to El Congo (bridge at Km 50) on Pan-American Hwy, US$1, then pick up the No 220 bus to the lake, US$0.45. Other buses to **Guatemala** may also stop at El Congo, so it's worth checking.

Taxi From **Santa Ana,** US$10.

Cerro Verde and Volcán Izalco
Bus From **Santa Ana**, bus No 248 goes to Santa Ana and Cerro Verde via El Congo. If you come from San Salvador wait for the bus at the other side of the main road, near the turn-off to Lake Coatepeque. The departures from Santa Ana are 0800, 1000 1100 and 1300. The bus arrives approximately 30 mins later at El Congo. The return bus leaves Cerro Verde at 1100, 1200, 1300, 1500, 1600 and 1730. The latest bus stops at El Congo and does not go all the way to Santa Ana. The journey between Cerro Verde at El Congo takes approximately 1 hr.

If you travel from **San Salvador** take the bus towards Santa Ana (No 205). Get off at the Shell petrol station at El Congo, cross the bridge that goes over the highway and catch the No 248 at the junction from Santa Ana. If you come from the west take the bus from Esso petrol station beween Izalco and Ateos that leads to Santa Ana and get off at junction 14 km below Cerro Verde summit and wait for No 248 that comes from El Congo.

Santa Ana and around

El Salvador's second city

Santa Ana (altitude 776 m, population 245,421) is 55 km from San Salvador and capital of its department. The basin of the Santa Ana volcano is exceptionally fertile, producing large amounts of coffee, with sugar cane coming a close second. The city, named Santa Ana La Grande by Fray Bernardino Villapando in 1567, is the business centre of western El Salvador.

There are some fine buildings: the neo-Gothic **cathedral**, and several other churches, especially **El Calvario**, in neoclassical style. Of special interest is the classical **Teatro de Santa Ana** ① *on the north side of the plaza, a guide (small charge) will show you round on weekdays, refer to the local press for performances*, originally completed in 1910, now in the latter stages of interior restoration and one of the finest theatres in Central America. The Fiestas Julias take place from 1-26 July.

Los Naranjos and around

Moving northeast of Juayúa, swirling up a scenic mountain road connecting Juayúa with Santa Ana, you arrive at Los Naranjos, a small traditional coffee village located at the mountain pass between Santa Ana and the Pilón volcanoes. The lines of wind-breaking trees preventing damage to coffee trees are particularly beautiful, while the high altitude makes the climate cool with the scent of cypress forests. A series of restaurants and small cabins for lodging has popped up in recent years and is an excellent option for cool climate and countryside relaxation.

At Km 82 on the Carretera Salcoatitán to Juayúa is **Parque y Restaurante La Colina** ① *T2452-2916, www.lacolinajuayua.com*, with hammocks, arts and crafts, and horse riding available. **Apaneca** is a short distance uphill from Sonsonate, see page 43.

Chalchuapa

About 16 km west of Santa Ana, on the road to Ahuachapán, lies Chalchuapa (altitude 640 m, population 96,727). President Barrios of Guatemala was killed in battle here in 1885, while trying to reunite Central America by force. There are

Santa Ana

To Metapán

To San Salvador (Carretera Panamericana)

To Sonsonate (Carretera Panamericana)

Buses to Cerro Verde

Parque Colón

Military Base

Campo Marte

To 8

N

200 metres
200 yards

To 5   To 3

Where to stay
Casa Frolaz **5**
Casa Verde **6**
Casa Vieja **7**
El Faro **1**

Sahara **4**
Villa Napoli **8**

Restaurants ⑦
Expresión **1**

Los Horcones **2**
Lover's Steak House **3**
Talitunal **4**

some good colonial-style domestic buildings. The church of Santiago Apóstol is particularly striking; almost the only one in El Salvador which shows strong indigenous influences (restored 1997-1998). Fiestas are on 18-21 July, Santiago Apóstol, and 12-16 August, San Roque.

Tazumal ruins next to the cemetery in Chalchuapa, are the tallest and probably the most impressive in El Salvador. They were built about AD 980 by the Pipil, with a 14-step pyramid. In 2004 the ruins suffered a partial collapse of the main pyramid due to the filtration of water which led to extensive excavations and application of new preservation techniques (getting rid of the old concrete) and many new discoveries were made. The excavations concluded in 2006. The site has been occupied since 5000 BC and in the **Museo Stanley H Boggs** ⓘ *Tue-Sun 0900-1600, T2408-4295*, you find artefacts found in Tazumal since the first excavations in the 1950s.

Casa Blanca Archaeological Site ⓘ *Km 78 Pan-American Hwy, T2408-4641, Tue-Sun 0900-1600, US$1*, just outside Chalchuapa, has several pyramids, ongoing excavations, and a museum that provides an insight into the archaeology of the area and information on indigo (*añil*) production. If you want to participate in the indigo workshop the cost is US$3. It's very interesting, educational and you can keep the products produced. Recommended.

Atiquizaya
The road continues 12 km west to Atiquizaya, a small, quiet town with one *hospedaje*, several good *pupuserías* (1600-2100) and **Restaurante Atiquizaya**, which can be found at the intersection with the main highway to Ahuachapán. At **Cataratas del Río Malacachupán** there is a beautiful 50-m-high waterfall cascading into a lagoon; it's a 1-km hike to get there. Nearby is **Volcán Chingo** on the Guatemalan border. Another attraction is **Aguas Calientes**, a hot spring that runs into the river and is excellent for a relaxing bath and for enjoying nature. It's a short ride from Atiquizaya, but bring a local guide.

Metapán
Texistepeque, 17 km north of Santa Ana on the road to Metapán, has an 18th-century baroque church, with fiestas on 23-27 December and 15 January. The town was one of the main areas for indigo production, and colonial processing plants known as *obrajes* exist all around the area. Visit the indigo workshop and museum of **Licenciado Marroquín** just out of town.

Metapán is about 10 km northeast of Lago de Güija and 32 km north of Santa Ana. Its colonial baroque **Catedral de San Pedro**, completed by 1743, is one of the very few to have survived in El Salvador. The altarpieces have some very good silver work, and the façade is splendid. The Fiesta de San Pedro Apóstol runs from 25-29 June. There are lots of easy walks with good views towards **Lago de Metapán** and, further on, **Lago de Güija**. If planning to walk in the hills near Metapán, seek local advice and do not walk alone.

Parque Acuático Apuzunga ⓘ *20 mins' drive from Metapán towards Santa Ana, T2483-8952, www.apuzunga.com*, is an adventure park by the Río Guajoyo, with fun pools, slides, zip-wires and a range of activities, including whitewater rafting and kayaking. There's a restaurant overlooking the river offering great views of the rafts shooting the rapids and the zip-wire over the water.

Reserva Nacional y Natural Montecristo

A mountain track from Metapán gives access to El Salvador's last remaining cloudforest, where there is an abundance of protected wildlife. It now forms part of El Trifinio, or the International Biosphere 'La Fraternidad', administered jointly by Guatemala, Honduras and El Salvador. The summit of **Cerro Montecristo** (2418 m) is the point where the three borders meet. At the Casco Colonial, a former finca, is a visitor centre, with a small museum and wildlife exhibits. Nearby is an **orchid garden** with over 100 species (the best time to see them in flower is early spring), an orchard and a camping ground in the forest. The views are stunning, as is the change seen in flora and fauna with the altitude. This highest elevated part is closed for visitors during the mating and reproduction season of the animals (31 May to 31 October).

Park information 20 km from Metapán to the park. Park employees (*guardabosques*) escort visitors and a permit is obtained (via fax or email) through MARN (Ministry of Environment) in San Salvador, T2267-6259 (with Patrimonio Natural and ask for Solicitud de Ingreso a Parque Nacional Montecristo). You need to fill out a form and pay US$6 per person. A 4WD is necessary in the wet season (mid-May to mid-October). To hire a 4WD and driver, contact Sr Francisco Xavier Monterosa, Calle 15 de Septiembre Casa 40, T2402-2805/T7350-1111 (mobile). The trails to the summit take four hours. Camping is permitted, with three campsites inside the park, spacious and clean, under the pine trees, with toilets, barbecue grills and picnic benches and tables. An overnight stay is needed if you want to reach the summit; worthwhile to fully appreciate the dramatic changes in vegetation as you climb from 800-2400 m above sea level.

Listings Santa Ana and around *map p55*

Where to stay

Santa Ana
Many hotels close their doors from 2000, so arrive early if you can.

$$$-$$ Villa Napoli
Quinta 'del Moral', Km 62-63 Cra Antigua a Santa Ana, T7808-0831, www. villanapoli-elsalvador.com.
As the name suggests, this hospitable and highly recommended B&B is Italian-owned. Service is warm and typically Mediterranean with an emphasis on client satisfaction. Rooms are simple, homely and comfortable, complete with local artwork, cable TV, a/c, and Wi-Fi; some have special discount rates for multiple nights. There is also a pool.

$$ Sahara
3 Calle Pte y 10 Av Sur, T2447-8865.
This older hotel has adequate and comfortable rooms with good service,

but it's a little overpriced. Popular for receptions and other events.

$$-$ Casa Verde
7a Calle Pte, entre 8 y 10 Av Sur, 25 Santa Ana, T7840-4896, www.hostalcasaverde.com.
An interesting 1940s house converted to a hostel. Rooms are clean and spacious and boast gallons of hot water. Dorms feature sturdy beds and unisex bathrooms. There are 2 kitchens with free coffee and water, Wi-Fi, lounge room with wide-screen TV and movies, 3 courtyards and a grill. As if that wasn't enough, there's a large pool and a roof terrace with panoramic views. Highly recommended.

$ Casa Frolaz
29 Calle Pte 42-B between 8 and 10 Av Sur, T2440-5302, www.casafrolaz.blog.com.
Beautiful and clean hostel with art, paintings, history books and a friendly reception, hot showers, tropical garden with hammocks and barbecue. Very popular with backpackers, constantly recommended.

$ Casa Vieja
9a Av Sur 10, T7757-1145.
This humble guesthouse has a patio, Wi-Fi and shared kitchen. Rooms are definitely no frills, but clean, spacious and comfortable, and the chilled out family atmosphere is definitely a winner. The owner Luis is very helpful and friendly.

$ El Faro I
14 Av Sur 9 entre 9 y 11 Calle Pte, T2447-7787, www.hoteleselfaro.com.
El Faro has 14 simple, economical rooms equipped with cable TV. Part of a local hospitality empire that includes

5 different establishments throughout the region, including lakeside accommodation; see their website for more details.

Los Naranjos and around

$$$ Los Naranjos Town Houses
Av 3, T7771-1484, losnaranjostownhouses@gmail.com.
Nestled among the trees and built from wood and stone, 4 unique and cosy countryside houses. Each has their own kitchen, cable TV and access to the tropical garden. Some enjoy great mountain views from their balconies.

$$$-$ Paso del Alaska Resort
Cra Santa Ana-Sonsonate Km 83, Vía Los Naranjos, T7731-7030, www.pasodelaalaska.com.
A great option for families and lovers of the outdoors, Paso de Alaska is an adventure tourism centre offering a host of activities including climbing walls, canopy tours, horse riding and hiking. Lodging includes comfortable cabins, apartments and tents. Their restaurant is reasonably popular too. Day-trippers welcome.

Metapán and around

$$$ Villa Limón
T2442-0149, www. hostalvillalimonmetapan.com. 30 mins' drive up very rough road (4WD only) northwest of Metapán.
Cosy, clean rooms in wooden *cabañas*, and a campsite in beautiful mountainside location, with huge zip-wires over the pine forests. Amazing views over Metapán, to lakes and volcanoes beyond. Full board, or bring your own food, advanced reservation essential; guided walks to nearby

waterfalls, and horse riding available. Recommended.

$$$-$$ Copa Cabana Aventura
Lotificación Loma Linda, T2402-0750,
www.copacabanametapan.com.
Enjoying fine vistas from its hilltop perch above Metapán, Copa Cabana offers comfortable rooms with shared balconies and a pool. Their restaurant serves *comida típica*.

$$ San José
Cra Internacional Km 113, Metapán,
near bus station, T2442-0556,
www.hoteleselsalvador.com.
This modern option has generic quarters with a/c, cable TV, safe parking and a restaurant.

Restaurants

Restaurants close quite early, between 2000 and 2100. *Comedores* are usually cheap and good value or try the food stalls beside the plaza or in front of the cathedral. Look for excellent pineapples in season.

$$ Los Horcones
On main plaza next to the cathedral.
Like a jungle lodge inside, with pleasant balcony dining and good cheap meals.

$$ Lover's Steak House
21 Calle Ote, entre Av Independencia y 3a
Av Sur, Barrio San Miguelito.
A very popular and long-standing place. Great value, recommended.

$$ Talitunal
5 Av Sur 6. Mon-Sat 0900-1900.
Vegetarian, attractive, good lunch, owner is a doctor and expert on medicinal plants.

$ Expresión
11 Calle Pte 20, between Av 6 and 8,
T2440-1410, www.expresioncultural.org.
A great little coffee bar, restaurant, bookshop and internet café, with occasional art exhibitions. The owner, Angel, speaks English. An obligatory stop. Recommended.

Chalchuapa
Several cheap and informal eateries with good-quality meals can be found around charming Parque Central.

$$ Los Antojitos
Calle Ramón Flores 6.
Good meals.

Metapán
Just before entering Metapán, 50 m off the highway, at the rim of the Lagunita Metapán, there are a couple of places with an international menu offering good fish from the lake, including **La Cocina de Metapán**, T2423-0014, which also has a pool and terrace. Both have a/c.

$$-$ Balompie
Opposite church on main square,
T2402-3567.
Upstairs restaurant, nice balcony, serves good-value mix of meat, seafood, pasta and snacks. Also serves the football stadium behind.

Transport

Bus No 201 from Terminal del Occidente, **San Salvador**, US$1-1.25, 1 hr, every 10-15 mins, 0400-1830. To **La Libertad**, take 'autopista' route bus to San Salvador and change buses in Nueva San Salvador. Buses (**Melva**, **Pezzarossi** and others) leave frequently from 25 Calle Pte y 8 Av Sur, T2440-3606, for

Guatemala City, full fare as from San Salvador, 4-4½ hrs including border stops. Alternatively, there are local buses to the border for US$0.45; they leave from the market. Frequent buses to **Metapán** and border at **Anguiatú**. No 238 follows a beautiful route to **Juayúa**; see also Border crossing box, page 111.

Atiquizaya
Bus There are frequent buses to the river from the central park in Atiquizaya; buses No 202 and 456 from Terminal Occidente in **San Salvador**, 2 hrs, US$0.90. From **Santa Ana**, 45 mins, US$0.40. All Ahuachapán buses stop in the Parque Central.

Metapán
Bus and car From **Santa Ana** bus No 235, US$0.80, 1 hr. If driving **San Salvador**–Metapán, a bypass skirts Santa Ana. Bus No 211 to border at **Anguiatú**; see also Border crossing box, page 111.

Western
Pacific coast

South of the capital, the seamy, steamy, rough-and-ready port town and low-key resort of La Libertad is the gateway to El Salvador's western Pacific coast, including the famous Costa del Bálsamo, which takes its name from pain-relieving balsam, once a major export of the region. On the steep slopes of the departments of Sonsonate and La Libertad, scattered balsam trees are still tapped for their aromatic juices, but the region is better known for its epic surf. A string of fishing villages turned low-key beach towns invite casual exploration with their blend of quiet beaches, private resorts, rustic digs and crashing Pacific waves. Buses travel along the coast as far as the border with Nicaragua and the journey offers stunning views of the rugged volcanic landscape.

La Libertad

a popular, laid-back seaside resort, with great surf nearby

Just before Santa Tecla, a branch road turns south for 24 km to the fishing port of La Libertad (population 35,997), 34 km from San Salvador and just 25 minutes from the Comalapa International Airport. Despite its reputation for sketchiness, and being none too clean, this is a busy resort and the whole area has been remodelled. It now has an amphitheatre, soccer and basketball courts, and a Complejo Turístico where the old naval building once stood, with a *malecón* and several restaurants.

The pier is worth seeing for the fish market awnings and, when the fleet is in, for the boats hauled up out of the water along its length. The cemetery by the beach has tombstones painted in the national colours, blue and white. On the seafront are several hotels and restaurants. At a small plaza, by the **Punta Roca** restaurant, the road curves left to the point, offering fine views of La Libertad bay and along the coast. The market street is two blocks inland across from the central church. The coast to the east and west has good fishing, surfing and bathing. The beaches are black volcanic sand (which can get very hot).

Tip...
La Libertad gets very crowded at weekends and holidays. For overnight stays the beaches to the west of La Libertad are better.

Service can be off-hand. Dedicated surfers may wish to stay for a while, as the breaks at Punta Roca in Puerto La Libertad are rated among the best in the world. The season runs from November to April and the surf is excellent. Watch your belongings on the beach and don't stay out alone late at night.

The town holds an annual **Gastronomic Festival** in early December and has resurrected the tradition of *lunadas* (full-moon parties) in the dry season. Bonfires are lit on the beach, restaurants stay open late offering *comida típica*, and some places provide live music and themed nights.

Around La Libertad

Just a few kilometres east of La Libertad on the Carretera Litoral is **Parque Nacional Walter Deininger** ⓘ *run by the Ministry of Tourism, T2243-7835, www. elsalvador.travel, for more information contact ISTU on T2222-8000, www.istu.gob. sv, US$3.* There are rivers and caves, and the park is great for hiking. There is even a seed bank for endangered tree species, an array of medicinal plants and a nursery. The views are fantastic and it's a good way to learn more about the flora and fauna, guides are available upon request.

Listings La Libertad

Tourist information

There's a **tourist kiosk** (T2346-1634, Mon-Fri 0800-1600, Sat and Sun 0900-1300) in the modern white complex opposite the fish market pier. You can also find local information in Spanish at www.puertolalibertad.com.

Where to stay

$$$ AST Surf Hotel
Calle Principal Malecón, Punta Roca, T2312-5143, www.astsurfhotel.com.
Overlooking the break at Punta Roca, AST is one of El Salvador's finest surf

lodges. It has 7 boutique rooms with Wi-Fi, satellite TV, a/c and large beds; 4 of them have ocean views. Various packages are available. Built by surfers for surfers.

$$ Pacific Sunrise
Calle Obispo, entrance of La Libertad, T2346-2000, www.hoteleselsalvador.com.
Hotel with pool, restaurant and rooms overlooking the Obispo beach, which can be accessed via an ingenious pedestrian overpass. Good rates if more people share the rooms.

$$ Rick
Behind Punta Roca.
A well-established and well-worn old cheapie. It has clean, basic rooms with bath. Friendly, good value. Also has a restaurant.

Restaurants

There are cheap restaurants near the pier, in the market, and around Playa La Paz, Playa El Obispo and El Sunzal. An area with new buildings located where the old Marina used to be close to the pier now hosts a series of great seafood eateries.

$$ El Nuevo Altamar
4 Calle Pte, Playa La Paz, T2335-3235.
Good for seafood, steaks and bird.

$$ La Curva de Don Gere
East of the Faro mall at the entrance to La Libertad, T2335-34360.
Legendary place run by Geremias Alvarado with several outlets in El Salvador (and the US). One of the trademarks is their seafood cream chowder in huge sizes including king crab legs and other goodies.

$$ La Dolce Vita
Playa Las Flores, 200 m east of the Shell petrol station, T2335-3592.
Excellent seafood and pasta restaurant.

$$ Mariscos Freddy and La Marea
On the beach at Playa Obispo.
Good-value seafood restaurants.

$$-$ Punta Roca
5 Av Sur, T2335-3261. Mon-Fri 0800-2000, Sat and Sun 0800-2300.
Try the shrimp soup. Owned by American ex-pat Robert Rotherham, father of the national surf champion Jimmy Rotherham.

What to do

Surfing
Look for board rentals and surf lessons at hostels on the coast west of Puerto La Libertad. Also look at www.sunzal. com, which offers great surfing tours combined with photography by local photographer, El Vaquero.

Punta Roca
Restaurant in La Libertad, T2335-3261 www.puntarocarockets.com.
Owner Robert Rotherham (father of Surf Champion Jimmy Rotherham) runs surfboard rental, including boards for both pros and beginners (see website for details). He also arranges excursions including deep-sea fishing for up to 3 people, see www.puntaroca.com.sv (which features webcam of area, surf and weather report) for more information. English spoken. Recommended.

Transport

Bus The station for buses going down to Puerto La Libertad is now located at the 17th Av Sur at the intersection of Blv Venezuela by the general cemetery in San Salvador. The buses going to San Salvador from Puerto La Libertad leave from the terminal at the entrance of the city centre by the ball courts. Departures from Puerto La Libertad along the coast to **Sonsonate** at 0600.

For beaches around Acajutla and west, take the direct bus from Terminal de Occidente to Sonsonate and then on: No 285 to **Barra de Santiago**, No 28 to **Cara Sucia** and the border and No 252 to **Acajutla**.

For **Costa del Sol**, **Zacatecoluca** and connections toward eastern beaches go from Terminal del Sur by San Marcos in San Salvador.

rugged black sand beaches, rocky outcrops and hidden coves

The Costa del Bálsamo unfolds between the ports of La Libertad and Acajutla. Playa Conchalío, 3 km west of La Libertad, is the first in the series of sandy stretches, closely followed by Playa El Cocal and Playa San Blas, which both cater to surfers, and Playa El Majahual, which also has good waves but is not very clean or safe. All of these beaches tend to be inundated with daytrippers at the weekend and during national holidays.

One of the most popular beaches for foreigners is ★Playa El Tunco. Offering easy access to two decent breaks – El Sunzal and La Bocana – it is renowned as one of the best surf spots in the area but is not so attractive for bathing. To get here take bus No 80 from La Libertad and get off at the turn-off where all the surfer hotels signs are posted (Roca Sunzal is the most visible one). It is then a short walk (a couple of blocks) to the seafront. Club Salvadoreño ⓘ www.clubsalvadoreno.com, and Club Tecleño ⓘ www.clubtecleno.com, both have their beach premises here and El Tunco itself has several hotels and restaurants. The nightlife can be buzzing, if decidedly low-key.

Further up the road at Km 43.5 is ★El Sunzal. Although the breaks are amazing at Sunzal, there have been reports of theft on the beach at dusk, so choose your accommodation carefully (such as the upmarket Casa de Mar, see Where to stay, below) or stay at El Tunco instead.

At Km 49.5 is Playa Palmarcito. This tiny and inviting beach is great for escaping the crowds and is good for novice surfers, as the breaks are not as violent as on other beaches. At Km 53.5 is ★Playa El Zonte, is another favourite among foreign tourists. It's a bit safer and quieter than El Tunco, being further away from La Libertad. The top-notch surf breaks has made El Zonte a place people stay longer than anticipated, and there are several well-established hotels with restaurant service. There are also several informal, cheap cafés and room rentals down at the beach.

The Carretera Litoral continues for a further 40 km or so to Acajutla past rocky bays, remote black-sand beaches and through tunnels. Take great care if you bathe along this coast, as it can be dangerous.

Acajutla and around

At the junction of San Julián, a short journey south from Sonsonate, the coastal road heads south to the lowland city of Acajutla (population 52,359), El Salvador's main port serving the western and central areas, 85 km from San Salvador (the port is 8 km south of the Coastal Highway). It is a popular seaside resort during the summer for Salvadoreans, but lodging in the village is not considered safe for foreigners. There are some good seafood restaurants with panoramic views.

The rocky beach of Los Cóbanos (14 km south of Acajutla via San Julián, bus from Sonsonate) is very popular with weekending Salvadoreans and has one of only two coral reefs along the entire Central American Pacific coast, making it a popular dive spot. Fishermen arrange boat trips; negotiate a price. José Roberto Suárez at **Los Cobanos Village Lodge** ⓘ *T2420-5248, sas_tun@hotmail.com,* speaks English and helprent boats and diving equipment.

The paved coastal road heads west running along the coast for 43 km before reaching the Guatemalan frontier at **La Hachadura**.

The black-sand beaches northwest of Acajutla at **Metalío** and Costa Azul (mostly full of private beach houses) and **Barra de Santiago** are recommended, although there are few public facilities. Barra de Santiago is a peninsula, 30 km west of Acajutla, and the beach is reached along a 7 km compact dirt road or across a beautiful lagoon. The entire area is a protected natural area in the process of being declared an ecological reserve to protect endangered species, including turtles, crocodiles and sea falcons. The *garza azul* (blue heron) is one of the amazing rare birds only found here. The mangrove is the third largest in El Salvador. This beach has an island named **El Cajete,** which has an archaeological site dating back to around AD 900. There are several pyramids but the area has not been excavated. **El Capricho Beach House** is a beautiful beachfront hotel here (see Where to stay, page 68).

★Parque Nacional El Imposible

Park entrance is US$6, payable at the gate. For more information contact Salvanatura office, 33 Av Sur 640, Col Flor Blanca, San Salvador, T2279-1515, www.salvanatura. org. Voluntary donation of US$4-5 a day. To get to the park, take the San Salvador–Sonsonate bus, and then bus No 259 to Cara Sucia. Pickups leave for the park at 1100 and 1400. From Guatemala and the border, regular buses heading for San Salvador pass through Cara Sucia from where you catch the 1100 and 1400 pickups.

So called because of the difficulty of transporting coffee through its ravines and down to the coast, today this 'impossibility' has helped preserve some of the last vestiges of El Salvador's flora and fauna on the rocky slopes and forests of the coastal **Cordillera de Apaneca**. Mule trains used to travel through the region, navigating the steep passes from which the park takes its name.

Among the mammals are puma, ocelot, agouti and ant bear; the birds include black-crested eagle, white hawk and other birds of prey, black and white owls, and woodpeckers. There is also a wide variety of reptiles, amphibians and insects, the greatest diversity in the country. There are eight different strata of forest, and over 300 species of tree have been identified. There is a small visitor centre, and rivers and natural pools to swim in. Trained naturalist guides from the nearby community of San Miguelito accompany visitors into the park, helping to identify season specific trails and routes, and pointing out interesting plants, animals and other attractions along the way.

Where to stay

Playa El Cocal

$$$ Punta Roca Surf Resort
T2300-0474, www.puntaroca.com.sv.
Owned by National Champion Jimmy
Rotherham, Punta Roca is a solid option
for surfers. Accommodation includes
simple rooms and bungalows.

Playa San Blas

$$$ Sabas Beach Resort
Cra Litoral Km 39, T2346-0029,
www.sabasbeachresort.com.
Nestled on the beach with easy access
to Punta Roca and El Sunzal, Sabas
resort is aimed squarely at surfers.
Rooms enjoy beach, ocean or mountain
views. There's a pool, bar and open-air
seafood restaurant.

Playa El Majahual

$$ Hotel y Restaurante Santa Fe
Cra Litoral Km 40.5, at the entrance to
Majahual beach, T2310-6508.
Safe, relaxed and functional place
with a pool and restaurant. Popular
with Salvadoreans.

Playa El Tunco

$$$ Tekuani Kal
Cra Litoral Km 42, T2355-6500,
www.tekuanikal.com.
Tekuani Kal is a modern boutique
option. With commanding ocean views
from their private balconies, rooms
are bright, colourful, spacious and
well-attired. There is also a pool, bar and
a fairly decent restaurant overlooking
the waves.

$$ Roca Sunzal
Km 42, T2389-6126,
www.rocasunzal.com.
One of the best hotels in El Tunco,
beautifully located in front of the
beach. Great views, pool, good food in
restaurant. The suites have artsy and
original decor. Great value and good
service. Recommended.

$$-$ Hotel Mopelia
T2389-6265,
www.hotelmopelia-salvador.com.
Owned by Frenchman Gilles, Hotel
Mopelia is a popular spot, with a bar and
pizzeria **Tunco Veloz**; see Restaurants
below. Accommodation includes
economical 'backpacker' rooms with
shared bath and more pricey 'suites' with
a/c. There is a pool.

$ La Guitarra
Cra Litoral Km42, T2389-6390,
www.surfingeltunco.com.
Fun place with a rocking beach bar.
Accommodation includes 18 rooms with
and without a/c, discounts for longer
stays, Wi-Fi.

$ Papayas Lodge
T2389-6231, www.papayalodge.com.
Family-run surf hostel. Clean rooms with
fans, use of kitchen and safe. Owned
by Salvadorean surf legend, Papaya.
Board sales and repair and surf classes.
Recommended.

$ Sol Bohemio
Cra Litoral Km39, T7262-0497,
www.solbohemio.com.
Offer reasonable rates, as do a couple
of the smaller hostels, such as **Barriles**.
They have a pool.

Playa El Sunzal

$$$$ B Boutique
Cra Litoral Km 45.9, Tamanique, T7210-9258, www.bboutiquehotel.com.
Crisp, classy, chic and minimalist, B Boutique enjoys unrivalled ocean views from its enviable cliff side perch. Rooms are calming, spacious and unbeatably stylish. When not admiring the sunset, guests can enjoy a private infinity pool, terrace and solarium. Recommended.

$$$$-$$$ Casa de Mar
www.casademarhotel.com.
This luxury hotel, located just in front of the breaks, is a good option if you want a splurge or to dine in their gourmet seafood restaurant, **Café Sunzal**, which has great food and panoramic views. Breakfast and Wi-Fi included.

$$$ Cielo Vista Hotel and Spa
Cra Litoral Km 43, T2374-2236, www.cielovistahotel.com.
Secluded and tranquil, Cielo Vista is a very special and romantic lodging set in beautiful lush grounds. It offers 5 luxury suites with individual themes, all impeccably furnished with 4-poster beds, private patios and jacuzzis. Spa treatments are available at extra cost. Stylish, luxurious and extravagant. Rates are per person. Recommended.

$$$-$$ Kayu Resort
Cra Litoral Km 43.5, T2389-6289, www.kayuelsalvador.com.
Perched above the beach, Kayu resort is an exclusive surf lodge with 7 cheery rooms, including 'economical' and 'luxury' options. There's an infinity pool and jacuzzi, both with calming ocean views. Breakfast included and tours available.

$$ Hostal Los Almendros
Cra Litoral Km 44.5, T7727 3194, www.go2losalmendros.com.
This cosy little surf hostel offers 8 reasonable, affordable rooms with fan and private bath. Food and tours are available and you can also enjoy ocean views and/or hammock time on the upper terrace.

$ Sunzal Point
Cra Litoral Km 44, T7327-9869, www.sunzalpoint.com.
Sunzal Point claims to be the oldest surf lodge in El Salvador, originally opened by the Angulo family in 1961. It has been renovated several times since then but remains a solid option for youthful travellers. It offers basic dorms and rooms, hammocks, kitchen, board rental, yoga classes, a party atmosphere and budget-friendly rates.

Playa Palmarcito

$$$ Atami Escape Resort
Km 49.5, T2355-7923, www.atami.com.sv.
Perched atop a cliff next to Palmarcito in 2 ha-grounds is this beautiful place with its own beach, 4 pools, plus saltwater pools and a water slide. Good rooms with a/c, cable TV and Wi-Fi. There's an expensive seafood restaurant, 2 bars and gardens. Day visitors US$20.

$ El Palmarcito
Km 50, T7942-4879, www.elpalmarcito.com.
This beachfront hotel offer surf lessons and board rental. There's also a restaurant.

Playa El Zonte

$ Esencia Nativa
T7737-8879, www.esencianativa.com.
Run by surfer Alex Novoa, with cheap
rooms, dorm and pool. Popular
restaurant serves range of options,
including great veggie food and is busy
at weekends. Surfing lessons and board
rentals available. Popular with surfers.

$ Horizonte Surf Camp
T2323-0099,
saburosurfcamp@hotmail.com.
Simple bungalows, some with a/c,
set in attractive gardens with a pool,
beachfront restaurant offering good food,
and board rental. Clean, good service.
Good choice for surfers. Room for up to 6
people on the 3rd floor. Great view.

$ La Casa de Frida Hotel
T2302-6068, www.lacasadefrida.com.
Lodging in cabins behind restaurant
with beachfront garden. Cosy place with
hammocks.

Acajutla and around

$$$$ La Cocotera Resort & Ecolodge
Barra de Santiago, T2245-3691,
www.lacocoteraresort.com.
Rates per person are fully inclusive
– full-board and airport transfers.
Small luxurious resort with thatched
bungalows on the beach and with
mangroves behind; pool, kayaks,
and tours available. Very peaceful.
Recommended.

$$ Los Cóbanos Village Lodge
Cra Acajutla, turn right at
Restaurant Marsolie, T2420-5248,
www.loscobanos.com.sv.
Beachfront cabins with pool and
restaurant. Scuba diving, surfing, fishing
on offer. TV and internet available.

$$-$ El Capricho Beach House
Barra de Santiago (same owners as
Ximena's), take direct bus No 285 to La
Barra de Santiago, which departs twice
daily from Sonsonate, or bus towards
border and pickup from turn-off, T2260-
2481, www.ximenasguesthouse.com
(under Capricho).
Beautiful beach and located in a wildlife
reserve, close to mangroves and the tip
of the peninsula. Clean rooms with bath
and a/c, cabin with dorms and ceiling
fan. Tours of the mangroves, fishing, surf
lessons and board rental all available.
Transport from the capital and tours to
Parque Nacional El Imposible available. A
safe place. Recommended.

Parque Nacional El Imposible

$$ Hostal El Imposible
T2411-5484.
With restaurant/bar area, pool and small
trail. 5 cabins sleeping 2-6 people have
private bath, hot water and small terrace,
also restaurant service. Information from
Salvanatura in San Salvador, T2279-1515.
www.salvanatura.org.

Restaurants

El Sunzal
Around the Sunzal area are several very
good restaurants, such **Hola Beto's**, **Las
Pamas Mirador** and **La Curva de Don
Gere**. All have beautiful vistas along
the coast.

$$ Café Sunzal
Km 43.5 Cra, T2389-6019,
www.cafesunzal.com.
Great seafood and steak house, exquisite
international cuisine. Excellent views
over El Sunzal beach.

Playa Palmarcito

$ Restaurante Las Palmas
Just in front of the beach.
Great meals and low prices.

Playa San Blas and Playa El Tunco

Tunco is on the rise and new places keep popping up.

$$ Hotel and Restaurante Roca Sunzal
Delicious seafood and a very good bar. All with an excellent beachfront location. Recommended.

$$ Hotel Mopelia
See Where to stay, above.
This place has a pizzeria and their well-stocked bar is open all week.

$$-$ La Bocana
In front of the Tunco (pig).
Owned and operated by Luis who's very friendly. Beachfront, offering great view from 2nd storey. Good seafood, great value.

$ Dale Dale Café
Behind Roca Sunzal.
Coffee shop serving delicious brownies, muffins and coffee to go with it.

$ Erika
T2389-6054.
Run by owner Amelia Hernández. Very popular with the locals. 2nd-storey palm thatched place with great atmosphere.

El Zonte

$ Esencia Nativa
See Where to stay, above.
Run by charismatic Alex Novoa, Esencia Nativa has an innovative menu, including good veggie options and pizzas, served at the poolside. Folks in the know come down from the capital just to get a bite.

$ Horizonte Surf Resort
An attractive restaurant at the beachfront run by Japanese Saburo. The view from 2nd floor is especially lovely. Good value.

$ La Casa de Frida
El Zonte, T2253-2949, www. lacasadefrida.com.
A great restaurant located in a large beachfront garden dotted with tables and hammocks.

Transport

Acajutla and around
58 km from **Santa Ana**.

Bus No 207 from Terminal Occidente, **San Salvador** (US$2.80), or No 252 from **Sonsonate** (US$0.30).

Northern
El Salvador

The obscure archaeological site of Cihuatán may appeal to diehard ruin-seekers, but bohemian Suchitoto is the undisputed highlight of northern El Salvador. The town itself is a tranquil place to unwind and the surrounding countryside, punctuated by highland waterfalls and the vast blue expanse of Cerrón Grande reservoir, is worth exploring too. Towards the Honduran border, La Palma is framed by fragrant pine forests and the country's highest peak, El Pital. On the other side of the reservoir, Chalatenango is the gateway to some fairly remote and bucolic communities. From here, a backdoor route leads all the way to Perquín and the Honduran border in the east (see page 85).

North from San Salvador

archaeological site en route to Suchitoto

The old highway, Troncal del Norte (CA 4) used to be the only acess to the north from the capital, but has been replaced with a modern highway. This can be accessed from Boulevard de la Constitución, in the northeastern part of San Salvador, and swirls west around the Volcán de San Salvador towards the Pan-American Highway and branches out to Nejapa, Quezaltepeque and Apopa to the north. It is 2½ hours by car from San Salvador to La Palma, then 11 km to the border at El Poy; see page 78.

Apopa and Tonacatepeque
Bus 38 B from San Salvador to Apopa, US$0.35.

Marking the junction with the road to Quetzaltepeque (12 km), Apopa has been subsumed into San Salvador's metropolitan sprawl and few travellers stop here. A paved road runs east from here to Tonacatepeque, an attractive small town on a high plateau. It has a small textile industry and is in an agricultural setting; check out the charming park and the colonial church. There has been some archaeological exploration of the town's original site, 5 km away. A paved road from Tonacatepeque runs 13 km south to the Pan-American Highway, some 5 km from the capital. At the same junction, a highway runs north from the Pan-American Highway to Suchitoto.

Aguilares

From Apopa, it's 21 km to Aguilares, 4 km beyond which are the ruins of **Cihuatán** ⓘ *Tue-Sun 0900-1600*. The name means 'place of women' and was presided over by female royalty. This was the largest city in Mesoamerica during the Toltec period, when the city was surrounded by extended fortification measuring more than 10 sq km. The biggest archaeological site in the country has several tall pyramids, ball courts and *temazcales* (ritual saunas). For more information about the site, contact chief archaeologist Paul Amaroli at FUNDAR in San Salvador, T2235-9453, www.fundar.org.sv.

A road goes from Aguilares heading east to Suchitoto. If heading north, see page 76.

★Suchitoto

See also www.gaesuchitoto.com and www.suchitoto-el-salvador.com. For information in English, contact US citizen Roberto Broz who runs Hostel and Restaurant El Gringo; see Restaurants, below.

Suchitoto (population 24,786), meaning 'the place of birds and flowers' in Náhuatl, was founded by the Pipil more than 1000 years ago. In 1528 the capital was moved to Suchitoto for 15 years as the villa of San Salvador suffered attacks from local tribes. In 1853 an earthquake destroyed much of San Salvador and many affluent families moved to Suchitoto leaving a lasting impression on the town.

Today it is a small, very attractive colonial town with cobbled streets, balconied houses and an interesting church. It is one of the favourite tourist spots in the country, with cultural traditions kept alive by the many artists living and working there. Several hotels and restaurants offer fantastic views towards Suchitlán and Volcán Guazapa. More than 200 species of bird have been identified in the area, and white-tailed deer inhabit the local woods.

The town was almost completely deserted in the early 1990s after 12 years of civil war which severely affected the region – 90% of the population left, leaving Suchitoto a virtual ghost town. However, a cultural revival has stimulated a range of activities and events, and the town is now considered the cultural capital of the country. Life centres on the main plaza which every evening becomes a bustle of people wandering the streets. Suchitoto's telegraph poles have been decorated by artist Paulo Rusconi, and Parque San Martín, to the west of town, is dotted with modern sculptures, some made using materials left over from the war. Arts and cultural festivals with internationally renowned artists take place every February. Another local festivity is the *Palo Encebado*, a competition involving attempts to clamber to the top of long greasy poles, and the *cerdo encebado* where a pig smeared with lard is chased through town and is kept by the first person who manages to grab it.

The **Teatro de Las Ruinas** is almost fully restored and hosts concerts and events. Contact Sra Chavez, T2335-1086, for more information. **Iglesia de Santa Lucía** ① *Mon-Sat 0800-1200 and 1400-1600, all day Sun*, built in 1858 with wooden and hollow columns, has also been restored with a lot of stencil work inside. There is a splendid view from the church tower. **Casa Museo de Alejandro Cotto** ① *daily 0900-1200 and 1400-1600, US$4, guided tour in Spanish (T2335-1140)*, home of movie director Alejandro Cotto, is an interesting museum with more than 132 paintings of El Salvador's most renowned artists, collections of books and music instruments.

Around Suchitoto

A 30-minute walk north of town leads to the **Embalse Cerrón Grande** (also known as **Lago de Suchitlán**). **Proyecto Turístico Pesquero Puerto San Juan** is a harbour with boat shuttle services and a complex of restaurants, craft shops and cafés on the lake shore. This is the departure point for boat excursions across to remote areas in neighbouring Chalatenango, ask around and negotiate prices. Trips are available to five islands including **Isla de Los Pájaros**, which makes an interesting trip (one to 1½ hours).

Suchitoto

Where to stay 🛏
El Gringo Hostel **2**
El Tejado **5**
Hostel Los Sánchez **7**
Los Almendros de
  San Lorenzo **1**
Posada Alta Vista **3**

Posada de Suchitlán **4**
Posada Blanca Luna **8**
Villa Balanza **6**

Restaurants 🍴
Café El Obraje **1**
El Dorado **6**

El Gringo **2**
Los Almendros de
  San Lorenzo **4**
Lupita del Portal **3**
Villa Balanza **8**

Ferries cross the Embalse Cerrón Grande for San Luis del Carmen (25 minutes to San Luis, frequent departures all day), where there is **Comedor Carmen**, and buses to Chalatenango. The ferry also makes a stop at the small village of **San Francisco Lempa**.

Los Tercios, a waterfall with striking, gigantic, black, hexagonal-shaped basaltic columns, can be reached by car, foot and by *lancha*. It is at its most impressive in the wet season when the full force of nature is on show. Walk 10-15 minutes from town down the very steep road towards the lake known as Calle al Lago de Suchitlán. Lifts are available for about US$2-3 if you can't face the steep climb back to town afterwards, ask around. At the lake shore, where there are *comedores*, ask for a *lanchero*. A *lancha* to the base of the trail to Los Tercios is US$5-6 (negotiable) and takes 10 minutes (ask the *lanchero* to point out the trail).

La Ciudad Vieja, one-time site of the capital, is 10 km from Suchitoto. An original Pipil town, it was taken over by the Spanish who made it their central base for 17 years before electrical storms, lack of water, and cholera forced them to flee. It is a private site but can be visited. There are plans for a museum and a café.

Boat trips go to lakeside villages associated with the FMLN in the civil war. On the road to Aguilares, 12 km away, a **Bosque de la Reconciliación** is being developed at the foot of Cerro de Guazapa. Contact **CESTA** ⓘ *T2213-1400, www.cesta-foe.org*, in San Salvador, or contact the park directly on T2213-1403 and speak to Jesús Arriola. Also, 3 km along this road is **Aguacayo** and a large church, badly damaged during the war.

Listings North of San Salvador *map p72*

Tourist information

Suchitoto

MITUR tourist office
Parque Centenario, T2335-1835. Mon-Fri 0800-1700, Sat-Sun 0800-1600.

Muncipal tourist office
Calle Francisco Morazán 7, next to the telephone office, T2335-1782, www.suchitoto-el-salvador.com. Daily 0800-1700.
Daily tours of the city centre, to Los Tercios waterfall and to Lake Suchitlán.

Where to stay

Suchitoto

$$$$ Los Almendros de San Lorenzo
4 Calle Pte, next to police station, T2335-1200, www.hotelsalvador.com.
In a restored colonial house with exclusive rooms, suites and delightful gardens. Delicious meals in the restaurant (see Restaurants below); people come from the capital to lunch here at weekends. Art gallery **Pascal**, across the street, has great exhibits, textiles and handicrafts (same French owner).

$$$$-$$$ Posada de Suchitlán
Final 4 Calle Pte, at the western end of town, T2335-1064, www.laposada.com.sv.

Colonial-style, beautifully tiled and decorated, excellent hotel and restaurant, including local speciality, *gallo a chichi* (chicken cooked in maize wine); stunning lake views.

$$$ El Tejado
3 Av Norte 58, Barrio Concepción, T2335-1769, www.eltejado suchitoto.net.
Beautifully restored colonial house with attractively furnished and spotless rooms, some with balcony; pool and gorgeous view of Lake Suchitlán. Pretty terrace restaurant.

$$ Hacienda La Bermuda
Km 34.8 Cra a Suchitoto, T2226-1839, www.labermuda.com.
Hotel and restaurant (see below) with frequent cultural activities, located just outside Suchitoto. Very atmospheric and full of history.

$$ Villa Balanza
North edge of Parque San Martín, T2335-1408. On the street behind the restaurant of the same name and 250 m to the right down the hill.
Small rooms but nicely furnished, with lovely views of lake from the hotel balcony.

$$-$ Posada Alta Vista
Av 15 de Septiembre 8, near the square, T2335-1645, www.hotelposadaaltavista.com.
Good rooms, although the cheaper ones can be hot. Helpful, friendly staff. Rooftop terrace with great view of the town.

$ El Gringo Hostel
Calle Francisco Morazán 27, T2327-2351, www.elgringosuchitoto.com.
A small and cosy hostel with just 2 private rooms and 1 shared dorm.

There's a simple shared kitchen, book exchange, chill out patio and Wi-Fi. Simple, economical, and definitely no frills. American-owned, as the name might suggest.

$ Hostal Los Sánchez
4a Calle Pte.
The Sanchez brothers have received lots of good reports for their kindness and hospitality. The rooms here are clean, simple, very spacious, and economical, and there's a good rooftop terrace with views over the town. Cable TV but no Wi-Fi.

$ Posada Blanca Luna
1a Av Sur y 1a Calle Ote 7, a block south of the church, T2335-1661, www.blancaluna.comoj.com.
This tranquil and slightly bohemian guesthouse has simple, economical rooms set around a small patio adorned with a hammock, tables and chairs. There is a small but functional communal kitchen, free drinking water and Wi-Fi at extra cost.

Restaurants

Suchitoto
Local specialities include *salporitas* (made of corn meal) and *chachamachas*. Try the *pupusas* in the market. Several eating options around the main plaza; many restaurants only open weekend evenings, especially during off season.

$$$ Los Almendros de San Lorenzo
4 Calle Pte, next to police station, Barrio El Centro (see Where to stay, above), T2335-1200, plebailly@hotel elsalvador.com.
Best restaurant in Suchitoto. Has a French chef, serves succulent meals and visitors come from San Salvador on weekends to dine here.

$$ El Dorado
*By Lake Suchitlán, T2225-5103,
www.gaesuchitoto.com.*
Bar and restaurant that hosts
frequent concerts.

$$ Hacienda La Bermuda
See Where to stay, above.
Colonial-style restaurant with pool and
cultural events.

$$ Lupita del Portal
*Parque Centenario, T2335-1679. Open
until midnight.*
The current hot spot. Serves gourmet
pupusas with home-grown herbs,
Salvadorean specialities and natural teas.
Owner René Barbón also runs **Suchitoto
Adventure Outfitters** from here, an
excellent tour operator (see What to
do, below).

$$ Villa Balanza
*Parque San Martín, T2335-1408,
www.villabalanzarestaurante.com.*
Rustic farm decor and antique bric-a-
brac, serving excellent local cuisine,
steaks and fish, and home-made fruit
preserves.

$ Café El Obraje
*Next to Santa Lucía church, T2335-1173.
Closed Tue.*
Clean and reasonably priced, with good
breakfast variety.

$ Restaurant El Gringo
*See Where to stay, above. Mon-Sat
0800-2000.*
Serves *pupusas* (normal and gourmet),
Tex/Mex and typical Salvadorean foods.
Famous for veggie burritos.

What to do

Suchitoto
Suchitoto Adventure Outfitters, *Calle
San Martín 4b, T7921-4216.* Excellent local
tours, including 5-hr horse-riding trip
up Volcán Guazapa to former guerrilla
camp, fascinating insights on war history
(US$35). Owner René Barbón speaks
excellent English and is extremely
knowledgeable and helpful.

Transport

Suchitoto
Bus To **Aguilares**, No 163 every 30
mins, 0500-1800, 30 mins. Regular buses
(No 129) from Terminal Oriente, **San
Salvador**, beginning at 0330. The bus
stops at the market and leaves town for
the capital from 3 Av Norte. To **Ilobasco**
by dirt road, 0800 and 1000, returning
1230 and 1430.

Ferry Cross the Embalse Cerrón
Grande (Lago de Suchitlán) for **San
Luis del Carmen** (25 mins to San Luis,
frequent departures throughout the
day, will leave whenever full, cars US$8,
foot passengers US$1) where there is
Comedor Carmen, and buses linking to
Chalatenango. Small *lanchas* also make
the short crossing from San Juan to San
Francisco Lempa on the north shore,
with onward buses to Chalatenango,
US$5 for the whole boat (up to
approximately 10 passengers).

a delightful little town

Highway 4 continues north from Aguilares, passing the western extremity of the Cerrón Grande reservoir. A branch to the east skirts the northern side of the reservoir to Chalatenango (population 30,808, altitude 450 m), capital of the department of the same name.

It is the centre of an important region of traditional livestock farms. It has a good market and several craft shops; for example, **Artesanías Chalateca**, for bags and hammocks. The weekly horse fairs, where horses, saddles and other equipment are for sale, are very popular. The town's annual fairs and fiestas are on 24 June and 1-2 November.

Rural Chalatenango is mainly agricultural and has many remote villages; there are a number of non-governmental organizations working in the area.

Listings Chalatenango

Where to stay

$ La Ceiba
1a Calle Pte, near 5a Av Norte, behind the military fort, Barrio Las Flores, T2301-1080.
Basic rooms with shower and bath and a/c in a quiet corner of town.

Restaurants

There are several restaurants to choose from including:

$$$-$ Rinconcito El Nuevo
Next to the military fort.
Good restaurant with an à la carte menu as well as *pupusas*. Check out bizarre collection of old sewing machines, irons, typewriters and other knick-knacks on display in the adjacent colonnade.

Transport

Bus No 125 from Oriente terminal, **San Salvador**, US$2, 2½ hrs.

La Palma and around

charming village in pine-clad mountains, and well worth a visit

The main road continues north through Tejutla to La Palma (altitude 1100 m, population 12,235). It is famous for its local crafts, particularly brightly painted wood carvings and hand-embroidered tapestries. Also produced are handicrafts made from clay, metal, cane and seeds. There are a number of workshops in La Palma where you can see handicrafts being made and buy some (see box, opposite). The Fiesta del Dulce Nombre de María takes place mid- or late February.

The artists' village of **La Palma**, in a pine-covered valley under Miramundo mountain, is 84 km north of the capital 10 km south of the Honduran frontier. Here, in 1971, the artist **Fernando Llort** 'planted a seed' known as the *copinol* (a species of the locust tree) from which sprang the first artists' cooperative, now called **La Semilla de Dios** (Seed of God). The copinol seed is firm and round; on it the artisans base a spiritual motif that emanates from their land and soul.

The town and its craftspeople are now famous for their work in wood, including exotically carved *cofres* (adorned wooden chests), and traditional Christmas *muñecas de barro* (clay dolls) and ornamental angels. Wood carvings, other crafts and the designs of the original paintings by Llort, are all produced and exported from La Palma to the rest of El Salvador and thence worldwide.

In 1971 the area was almost exclusively agricultural. Today 75% of the population of La Palma and neighbouring San Ignacio are engaged directly or indirectly in producing handicrafts. The painter **Alfredo Linares** (born 1957 in Santa Ana, arrived in La Palma 1981 after studying in Guatemala and Florence) has a gallery in La Palma, employing and assisting local artists. His paintings and miniatures are marketed abroad, yet you will often find him working in the family pharmacy next to the gallery. Many of La Palma's images are displayed on the famous Hilasal towels. If you cannot get to La Palma, visit the shop/gallery/workshop of Fernando Llort in San Salvador, **Arbol de Dios**.

Twenty kilometres from the capital is the indigenous town of **Panchimalco**, where weaving on the loom and other traditional crafts are being revived. Many Náhuatl traditions, customs, dances and the language survived here as the original indigenous people hid from the Spanish conquistadors in the valley beneath the Puerta del Diablo (now in Parque Balboa). In 1996 the painter Eddie Alberto Orantes and his family opened the **Centro de Arte y Cultura Tunatiuh**, named after a Náhuatl deity who is depicted as a human face rising as a sun over a pyramid. The project employs local youths (from broken homes, or former addicts) in the production of weavings, paintings and ceramics.

In the mountains of western El Salvador, villages in the coffee zone, such as **Nahuizalco**, specialize in weaving henequen, bamboo and reed into table mats and wicker furniture. There are also local artists like Maya sculptor **Ahtzic Selis**, who works with clay and jade. East of the capital, at **Ilobasco** (60 km), many ceramic workshops produce items including the famous *sorpresas*, miniature figures enclosed in an egg shell. In the capital there are craft markets, and throughout the country, outlets range from the elegant to the rustic. Everywhere, artists and artisans welcome visitors into their workshops.

The picturesque village of **San Ignacio**, 6 km north of La Palma, has two or three small *talleres* producing handicrafts (20 minutes by bus, US$0.10 each way).

San Ignacio is the departure point for buses ascending a safe but steep road leading up to the highest mountain of El Salvador, El Pital (2730 m). As you reach the pass below the mountain top, the road branches to **Las Pilas** to the left and **Miramundo** to the right. Both Miramundo and Las Pilas have small agricultural communities, specializing in organic crops. The extensive cabbage fields combined with the pine-clad mountains make for beautiful vistas.

If you take the road from the summit to the right, you end up in Miramundo which gives a view of pretty much all El Salvador. On clear days you can see almost all the volcanoes in the country, including Volcán Pacaya and Volcán Agua in Guatemala. This is no doubt the best view in the country.

Border with western Honduras

The road continues north to the border at **El Poy**, for western Honduras; see box, page 112. From Citalá, there is a small town with a colonial church and a potent war history (you still see bullet holes in the walls of the houses on street corners). One kilometre west off the highway just before El Poy, an adventurous road leads to Metapán. Two buses daily take three hours to travel the 40 km, a rough but beautiful journey.

Listings La Palma and around

Where to stay

$$$$-$$$ El Pital Highland
East of San Ignacio at the edge of the Reserva Biologica El Pital, T2221-6954, www.elpital.com.sv.
Suitable for adventurous couples or families, El Pital Highland has 3 highland *cabañas* of various sizes, all equipped with chimneys for those chilly nights (do bring warm clothing too). There are also cheaper rooms. Rates include 3 meals. It's best to contact the lodge in advance of your visit.

$$$ Entre Pinos
San Ignacio, T2335-9312, www.entrepinosresortandspa.com.
1st-class resort complex, a/c, pool, cable TV, sauna and small shop.

$$$-$$ Hostal El Pital Lecho de Flores
Cantón Río Chiquito, southern edge of the Reserva Biological El Pital, T2313-5470, www.elpitallechodeflores.com.
Hostal El Pital has 6 *cabañas* built from stone or wood, each suitable for up to 4-6. There is a restaurant and various packages to cover costs of lodging, food and guides.

$$ Hotel La Palma
Troncal del Norte, 84 km Cra, La Palma, T2335-9012, www.hotellapalma.com.sv.
32 large rooms, clean, with bath. Friendly, with good restaurant, beautiful gardens, good pool, ceramics workshop, parking and petrol station. Also runs guided walks around local trails, including El Tecomate, Río Nunuapa and Los Pozos. Recommended.

$ Casa de Huéspedes Las Orquídeas
Las Pilas.
Run by a local farming family. Ask for a
guided trip to the mountain top nearby,
for an unrivalled panoramic view and
free peaches.

$ Hostal Miramundo
Miramundo, T2219-6251,
www.hotelmiramundo.com.
Nice rooms with hot water. A
restaurant, great food and great views.
Recommended.

$ Las Praderas de San Ignacio
San Ignacio, a few kilometres before
the border, T2350-9330, www.
hotelpraderasdesanignacio.com.
Cabins, beautiful gardens and an
inexpensive restaurant.

Restaurants

In Ignacio, there are many local
comedores, including Comedor
Elisabeth, which offer delicious *comida*
a la vista including fresh milk, cheese
and cream.

$ El Poyeton
Barrio San Antonio, 1 block from church,
La Palma.
Reliable, serves simple dishes.

$ La Estancia
Calle Principal, La Palma, T2335-9049.
Open 0800-2000.
Good menu, useful bulletin board.

Shopping

Handicrafts
There are more than 80 arts and crafts
workshops in La Palma; www.lapalma
elsalvador.com, provides a complete
list of all the workshops and how to
contact them. Many workshops have
come together and formed a **Placita**
Artesanal, an artisan market, which is
located by the Catholic church on the
central plaza.
Cooperativa La Semilla de Dios, *Plaza*
San Antonio. The original cooperative
founded by Fernando Llort in 1971. It has
a huge selection of crafts and paintings
and is helpful.
Gallery Alfredo Linares, *Sr Linares'*
house (if gallery is unattended, ask
in the pharmacy), T2335-9049. Daily
0900-1800. Friendly well-known artist
whose paintings sell for US$18-75.
Recommended.
Palma City, *Calle Principal behind church.*
Sra Alicia Mata is very helpful and will
help find objects, whether she stocks
them or not (wood, ceramics, *telas*, etc).

Transport

Bus From **San Salvador**, Terminal de
Oriente, No 119, US$2.25, 3 hrs, last
bus at 1630. To La Palma from Amayo,
crossroads with Troncal del Norte (main
highway to San Salvador), and E-W road
to **Chalatenango**, bus No 119 every 30
mins, US$1.35.

Eastern
El Salvador

The towns of eastern El Salvador maintain a rich festival life and strong craft traditions: Ilobasco is a pottery centre and San Sebastián specializes in textiles. The ancient town of San Vincente has history and colonial airs whilst San Miguel is a small, hot, rapidly growing city and transport hub. To the north, don't miss Perquín, a special little mountain town steeped in arresting scenery and legends of the revolution. To the south, on the coast, the port town of La Unión is not a destination in itself, but the jumping off point for the mellow pirate isles of Meanguera, Zacatillo and Conchagüita.

East from San Salvador

towards El Salvador's rural heartland

There are two roads to the port of La Unión (formerly known as Cutuco) on the Gulf of Fonseca: the Pan-American Highway, 185 km through Cojutepeque and San Miguel (see page 82); and the coastal highway, also paved, running through Santo Tomás, Olocuilta, Zacatecoluca and Usulután.

The Pan-American Highway is dual carriageway out of the city, but becomes single carriageway for several kilometres either side of Cojutepeque – sections that are twisty, rough and seem to induce some very bad driving.

At San Martín, 18 km from the capital, a paved road heads north to Suchitoto, 25 km on the southern shore of the Embalse Cerrón Grande, also known as Lago de Suchitlán. At Km 34.8 is **Hacienda La Bermuda**, see page 74.

Cojutepeque
The capital of the Department of Cuscatlán, Cojutepeque (population 50,315) is 34 km from San Salvador and the first town on the Pan-American Highway encountered when heading east. There is a good weekly market. The town is famous for cigars, smoked sausages, *quesadillas* and tongue, and its annual feria

on 29 August has fruits and sweets, saddlery, leather goods, pottery and headwear on sale from neighbouring villages, and sisal hammocks, ropes, bags and hats from the small factories of Cacaopera (Department of Morazán). There is also a **sugar cane festival** on 12-20 January. Lago de Ilopango is a short trip to the southwest.

Cerro de las Pavas, a conical hill near Cojutepeque, dominates **Lago de Ilopango** and offers splendid views of wide valleys and tall mountains. Its shrine of **Our Lady of Fátima** draws many pilgrims every year (religious ceremonies take place here on 13 May).

Ilobasco

From **San Rafael Cedros**, 6 km east of Cojutepeque, a 16-km paved road north to Ilobasco (population 61,510) has a branch road east to Sensuntepeque at about Km 13. The surrounding area, devoted to cattle, coffee, sugar and indigo, is exceptionally beautiful. Many of Ilobasco's population are workers in clay; although some of its decorated pottery is now mass-produced and has lost much of its charm, this is definitely the best place to buy pottery in El Salvador. Check out miniature *sorpresas*, delicately shaped microscopic sceneries the size of an egg (don't miss the naughty ones). Try **Hermanos López** ① *entrance to town*, or **José y Víctor Antino Herrera** ① *Av Carlos Bonilla 61, T2332-2324, look for the 'Kiko' sign*, where there are fine miniatures for sale. The annual fiesta is on 29 September.

San Sebastián

Four kilometres from the turning to Ilobasco, further south along the Pan-American Highway at **Santo Domingo** (Km 44 from San Salvador), a paved road leads for 5 km to San Sebastián (population 14,411), where colourfully patterned cloth hammocks and bedspreads are made. You can watch them being woven on complex looms of wood and string. Behind **Funeraria Durán** there is a weaving workshop. Sr Durán will take you past the caskets to see the weavers. The **Casa de Cultura**, about 50 m from the plaza, will direct you to weaving centres and give information on handicrafts. Before buying, check prices and beware of overcharging. Market day is on Monday.

San Vicente

Founded in 1635, San Vicente (population 53,213) is 61 km from the capital and lies a little southeast of the Highway on the Río Alcahuapa, at the foot of the double-peaked **Volcán San Vicente** (or **Chinchontepec**), with very fine views of the Jiboa valley to the west. The town has a lovely setting and is a peaceful place to spend a night or two. Its pride and joy is **El Pilar** (1762-1769), the most original church in the country. It was here that the local chief, **Anastasio Aquino**, took the crown from the statue of San José and crowned himself King of the Nonualcos during the rebellion of 1832.

El Pilar stands on a small square 1½ blocks south of the Parque Central. On the latter is the **cathedral**, whose nave is draped with golden curtains. In the middle of the main plaza is a tall, open-work **clock tower**, quite a landmark when descending the hill into the city. Three blocks east of the main plaza is the *tempisque* tree under which the city's foundation charter was drawn up. The tree was decreed a national monument on 26 April 1984. There's an extensive market area a few blocks west of the centre and hammock sellers are on nearby streets. An army barracks takes up an entire block in the centre. There's a small **war museum**; ask the FMLN office here or in San Salvador. Carnival day is 1 November.

Around San Vicente

Three kilometres southeast of the town is the **Balneario Amapulapa** ① *T2393-0412, US$0.80 entry and US$0.90 parking charges, a Turicentro.* There are three pools at different levels in a wooded setting. The tourist police patrols here and lately it's been considered a safe place for tourists, although women should not walk to the area alone. It's reached by bus No 177 from Zacatecoluca bus station, and by pickup from the San Vicente bus station.

Laguna de Apastepeque ① *T2389-7172*, near San Vicente off the Pan-American Highway, is small but picturesque. Take bus No 156 from San Vicente, or No 499 from San Salvador. Ask in San Vicente for guides for climbing the San Vicente volcano.

San Miguel

Set at the foot of the Volcán San Miguel (Chaparrastique), which last erupted in 1976 but has shown activity ever since, San Miguel (population 218,410) is the third largest city in El Salvador, 136 km from San Salvador. Apart from its huge carnival (see below), San Miguel is not a place you're likely to want to linger;

San Vicente

To Pan American Highway & San Salvador

5 C Pte · 5 C Ote/Domingo Santos

1 Av Norte · 2 Av Nte

Cambio León

F A Figueroa/3 C Pte · Dr A J Cañas

Av Canónigo R Lazo

Clock Tower · Tempisque Tree

Cathedral

Lic Hernán Miranda · Daniel Díaz

Av María de los Angeles · Av José María Cornejo

Bus to Apasteque

Alcaldía

Army Barracks

Gobernación

1 de Julio 1823

Av Inocente Marín · Av F C Cañadas · Av Max Ramírez · Av Pres M A Molina y Cañaso · Av Ana Guerra de Jesús · Av Cayetano Molino Quiroz

Lic Basilio Meriño · Alberto de Merino

El Pilar

Indalecio Miranda · Juan C Segovia

N

200 metres
200 yards

Where to stay 😊
Central Park **1**

there are traffic-clogged streets, stinking gutters, a hot, sticky climate and few conventional tourist attractions.

The capital of its department, the town was founded in 1530 as a military fortress by Don Luis de Moscoso. It now has one of the fastest growing economies in Central America, thanks partly to *remesas* (money received from family members who have emigrated to the US), as this part of the country experienced heavy migration both during and after the civil war. The town has two shady plazas: **Parque David J Guzmán**, containing the bare 18th-century cathedral, and the adjacent **Plaza Barrios**, flanked by overflowing market stalls. The city's **theatre** dates from 1909 and has been reopened in all its original glory.

The **Fiesta de la Virgen de la Paz** is on the last Saturday in November, and one of the biggest carnivals in Central America, known as **El Carnaval de San Miguel**, also takes place here. The free festival features parades and marching bands filing down Avenida Roosevelt to the city centre, from 1900 until late. For more information contact the **Comite de Festejos** ⓘ *T2660-1326*.

Listings East from San Salvador *maps p82 and p83*

Where to stay

San Vicente

$ Central Park
On Parque Central, T2393-0383.
Good, clean rooms, with bath, a/c and phone. Cheaper with fan, cheaper still without TV. Café and restaurant downstairs.

San Miguel
Most hotels are on the entrance roads, although there are plenty of cheap places near the bus station.

$$ Trópico Inn
Av Roosevelt Sur 303, T2682-1082, www.tropicoinn.com.sv.
Clean and comfortable, with reasonable restaurant, swimming pool, garden

San Miguel

200 metres
200 yards

Where to stay 🛏
King Palace 1

Trópico Inn 2

and safe parking for motorbikes. Recommended.

$ King Palace
Opposite the bus station.
Good breakfast.

Restaurants

Ilobasco
There are 2 pizzerias, several local *comedores*, a **Pollo Campero** and a **Taco Hut**.

$$ Restaurante Ricky
3 Av Sur.
The town's only real restaurant with à la carte dining.

San Vicente
The San Vicente Gastronomical festival is held on the last Sat of the month at the central park. Close to Hotel Central Park are **Pops** and **La Nevería**, for good ice cream.

San Miguel
Try *bocadillos de totopostes*, maize balls with either chilli or cheese; and *tustacos*, which are like small tortillas with sugar or honey. Both are delicious and traditional.

$ El Gran Tejano
4 Calle Pte, near the cathedral.
Great steaks.

$ Restaurant Perkin Lenca
Km 205.5 Cra a Perquín, T2680-4080, www.perkinlenca.com. Daily 0700-2000.
Part of the hotel of the same name, this restaurant serves traditional food.

Transport

Cojutepeque
Bus No 113 from Oriente terminal in **San Salvador** (US$0.80); buses leave from Cojutepeque on the corner of the plaza, 2 blocks from the main plaza.

San Sebastián
Bus No 110 from the Oriente terminal runs from **San Salvador** to San Sebastián (1½ hrs, US$1). There are also buses from **Cojutepeque**.

San Vicente
Bus No 116 from Oriente terminal, **San Salvador**, every 10 mins or so (1½ hrs, US$0.90). Returning to the capital, catch bus from the bus station, Av Victoriano Rodríguez y Juan Crisóstomo Segovia; outside the cathedral; or on the road out of town. To **Zacatecoluca**, No 177 (US$0.50) from bus station. Buses to some local destinations leave from the street that runs west to east through the market. You have to take 2 buses to get to **San Miguel** (see below), the first to the Pan-American Hwy, where there is a bus and food stop, then another on to San Miguel (US$1.50 total).

San Miguel
Bus Nos 301, 306 and 346 from Oriente terminal, **San Salvador** US$2.50, every 30 mins from 0500 to 1630, 2½ hrs. There are also 3 comfortable express buses daily, 2 hrs, US$5.

There are frequent buses to the Honduran border at **El Amatillo**, US$1; see also box, page 112. 4 buses, No 332A, daily to **Perquín**, from 0600-1240, 2¾ hrs, US$1.60. Direct to Tegucigalpa, with **King Quality Bus**, T2271-0307, www.kingqualityca.com, daily at 0830 and 1630, 6 hrs, US$35.

Several routes radiate outwards from San Miguel. A paved road runs south to the Pacific Highway. Go south along it for 12 km, where a road leads to Playa El Cuco (bus No 320 from San Miguel, US$1.50). A mainly paved, reasonable road goes to west to San Jorge and Usulután: leave the Pan-American Highway 5 km west of San Miguel, where the road passes hills and coffee plantations with good views of the San Miguel volcano.

Another route heads northeast to the small town of Jocorro, where the road splits with options to Honduras. Heading north, San Francisco Gotera leads to the Perquín crossing; east of Jocorro the road leads to the border crossing at El Amatillo (see box, page 112); and directly east from San Miguel lies La Unión, with connections north to El Amatillo.

San Francisco Gotera and around
The capital of Morazán Department can be reached directly from the Oriente terminal in San Salvador, or from San Miguel (bus No 328). There are places to stay (see Where to stay, below).

Beyond San Francisco, the road runs to **Jocaitique** (there is a bus) from where an unpaved road climbs into the mountains through pine forests to **Sabanetas**, near the Honduran border; see Border crossing box, page 112. Accommodation is available at Jocaitique and Sabanetas.

Northeast of San Francisco is **Corinto** ⓘ *20 mins north of the village on foot, just east of the path to the Cantón Coretito, open daily, take an early bus, No 327, from San Miguel, US$1,* which has two rock overhangs showing faint evidence of pre-Columbian wall paintings.

Ciudad Segundo Montes and around
Eight kilometres north of San Francisco Gotera is Ciudad Segundo Montes, a group of villages housing 8500 repatriated Salvadorean refugees (the community is named after one of the six Jesuit priests murdered at the Central American University in 1989). Schafic Vive is a small museum with information on the community. If you wish to visit contact **PRODETUR** ⓘ *T2680-4086,* for information. No formal accommodation is available.

Fourteen kilometres north of San Francisco is **Delicias de la Concepción**, where fine decorated hammocks and ceramics are made. The prices are good and the people are helpful; worth a visit. Buses every 20 minutes from San Francisco.

Perquín and around
Perquín (altitude: 1200 m, population: 3158) – meaning 'Road of the Hot Coals'– is 205 km from San Salvador and was the guerrillas' 'capital', and the scene of much military activity. War damage used to be visible around the town, but all is now peaceful and the scenery is very beautiful, surrounded by pine-topped

mountains. There is a small central square with a Casa de la Cultura, and post office. Opposite is the plain Iglesia Católica Universal Progresista, next to which is POLITUR, the very helpful and friendly police station. The tourist office is jointly run by **PRODETUR** and **Perkin Tours** travel agency ① *Final del Calle Principal, T2680-4086, www.prodeturperquin.tripod.com, Mon-Fri 0800-1700.*

The **Museo de la Revolución** ① *T7942-3721, daily 0800-1700, US$1.20, no photos or filming allowed, guided tours in Spanish, camping permitted, US$1*, clearly signposted from the plaza, has temporary exhibits as well as one on Archbishop Romero and all the gory details of his murder – nothing is spared. The museum, run by ex-guerrillas, is badly lit, but fascinating with photographs, propaganda posters, explanations, objects, pictures of the missing, and military paraphernalia. In the garden is the wreckage of an American-made helicopter, shot down by guerrillas in 1984. Sprawled like a piece of modern art, it would look at home in a contemporary art gallery. There is also a room where a recreated cabin shows the place from where the clandestine radio *Venceremos* broadcast their programmes during the war.

Behind the town is the **Cerro de Perquín** ① *US$0.25 to climb, it is advisable to bring a guide*. The views are fantastic with the town below nestling in the tropical scenery, green parrots flying through the pine trees, and the mountains stretching towards the border with Honduras. The **Festival de Invierno**, 1-6 August, is a mixture of music, exhibitions and film. Book accommodation in advance if you're planning to come for the festival. The **Festival de San Sebastián** is on 21-22 January, and the celebration of the **Virgen del Tránsito**, the patron saint of the church, takes place 14-15 August.

Nearby villages such as Arambala and El Mozote can be visited, or you can take a walking tour. At **El Mozote** is a memorial to a massacre that took place in 1981, during which more than 800 people, among them children and babies, were brutally murdered. Five kilometres west of Perquín is **Arambala**, which is slowly being rebuilt. Locals will give you a tour (free, but tips appreciated) of the town and church, which has been largely rebuilt since being destroyed by fire in the 1980s; a sad and deeply moving experience, well worth the effort. Opposite the church is a small crafts shop run by a local women's cooperative, some of whom are also guides. Near Perquín, turn-off 2 km south, are the park and trails of **Cerro Pelón**. Nearby is **El Llano del Muerto**, a tourist area of naturally heated pools and wells. North of Perquín, straddling the border with Honduras, is one of the few unpolluted rivers in the country. The people of Morazán are more reserved with strangers than in the rest of El Salvador. If travelling on your own, 4WD is advised.

Ruta de Paz run by **Perkin Tours** ① *T2680-4086, perkintours@yahoo.es, daily 0800-1700, 0800-2100 during the winter festival*, provides walks, culture and adventure tourism, and can organize accommodation. Tours last for between 25 minutes and two days, and are for one to 10 people. Ask for Serafín Gómez, who is in charge of the tours.

Santa Rosa de Lima

The shortest route from San Miguel to the Honduran border takes the Ruta Militar northeast through Santa Rosa de Lima (population 27,693) to the Goascarán bridge at El Amatillo, a total of 58 km on paved road; see the Border crossing box on page 112.

Santa Rosa is a charming little place with a wonderful colonial church set in the hillside. There are gold and silver mines, a market on Wednesday, and a curiously large number of pharmacies and shoe shops. The **FMLN** office has details about the **Codelum Project**, a refugee camp in Monte Barrios. The fiesta is on 22-31 August.

Listings Routes from San Miguel

Where to stay

San Francisco Gotera

$$-$ Hospedaje San Francisco
Av Morazán 29, T2654-0066.
Nice garden and hammocks.

Perquín and around

$$ Hotel Perkin Lenca
Km 205.5 Cra a Perquín, T2680-4080,
www.perkinlenca. com.
Cosy Swiss cabins with piping hot showers and thick blankets. Excellent meals in restaurant **La Cocina de Ma'Anita**, with panoramic terrace overlooking forested hills, daily 0700-1900. US owner Ronald organizes tours to El Mozote with former guerrilla guides, a bit grim but very moving.

$ Cocina Mama Toya y Mama Juana
At the entrance of Perquin village,
T2680-4045.
Small rooms with 3 beds and shared bath. Parking.

$ La Posada de Don Manuel
5 mins from Perquín at the bottom of the hill, CTE Perquín T2680-4037.
Previously called **El Gigante**, countless partitioned rooms that would probably

be noisy if full, but rarely are. Clean, with cold showers and meals. They have a highly recommended restaurant and organize tours with guides. Friendly.

Camping
It's possible to camp in the grounds of the **Museo de la Revolución**, near a crater formed by a 227-kg bomb dropped in 1981. Ask in the nearby *tiendas.*

Near the Río Zapo, **PRODETUR** (T2680-4311, prodeturperquin.tripod. com), has a great campsite with facilities, and there are guides who can give you a tour of the area. Good for both trekking and hiking. There is also a simple cabin for rent here.

Santa Rosa de Lima

$ Hospedaje Mundial
Near the market.
Basic rooms with fan. Friendly, lots of parking.

$ Recreo
2 blocks from town centre in front of police station and Telecom, 4 Av Norte, Barrio el Recreo, T2641-2126.
Basic fan rooms, noisy but friendly. Recommended.

Restaurants

Perquín and around

$ Antojitos Marisol
T2680-4063, near the church on the south side of the plaza. Open late.
Simple food.

$ La Cocina de Mi Abuela
At the entrance to town. T2502-2630.
Popular with locals with good, local dishes.

Santa Rosa de Lima

$$ Martina
Near the bridge.
Good food including *sopa de apretadores* for US$7.

Transport

Perquín and around
Bus From **San Miguel**, bus No 332A (2¾ hrs, US$1.50). The bus from Terminal Oriente in **San Salvador** (4½ hrs) is very crowded, luggage a hindrance. Bus or truck from **Cd Segundo Montes**. Transport back to Cd Segundo Montes or San Miguel may be difficult in the afternoons.

Car
If you're driving fill your tank before getting to Perquín because the last petrol station is 20 mins from the city and closes at 1700.

Santa Rosa de Lima
Bus To the Honduran border every 15 mins, US$0.50; see also box, page 112. Direct buses also to **San Salvador**, No 306, from 0400 until 1400, US$3.25, 3½ hrs.

La Unión

launching pad for remote Pacific islands

It is another 42 km from San Miguel to the port of La Unión (population 34,045), on the Gulf of Fonseca. The spectacular setting on the west shore of the gulf does little to offset the heat and the faded glory of this port town which handles half the country's trade. Shortly before entering the town, the Pan-American Highway turns north for 33 km to the Goascarán bridge at El Amatillo on the border with Honduras (see box, page 112). A project to inaugurate the modern port of La Unión is scheduled to happen in 2015. This huge project includes numerous foreign investments, such as a large Spanish tuna fish processing plant, with supporting infrastructure including new roads, hotels and a school running training in logistics and tourism.

Around la Unión
Conchagua is worth visiting to see one of the few old colonial churches in the country, and there is a good bus service from La Unión (No 382, US$0.10). The church was begun in 1693, after the original Conchagua had been moved to its

present site following repeated attacks on the island settlements by the English. There are fiestas on 18-21 January and 24 July.

There is also **Volcán Conchagua** (1243 m) which can be climbed but is a hard walk, particularly near the top where protective clothing is useful against the vegetation. It's about four hours up and two hours down, but you will be rewarded with superb views over Volcán San Miguel to the west and the Gulf of Fonseca, which is bordered by El Salvador, Honduras and Nicaragua (where the Cosigüina volcano is prominent) to the east. Alternatively, you can drive up via the community of Conchagita (4WD only).

In the Gulf of Fonseca are the Salvadorean islands of **Isla Zacatillo**, **Isla Conchagüita** and the largest, **Isla Meanguera** (about 4 km by 7 km). English and Spanish pirates occupied Isla Meanguera in the late 1600s, and international claims remained until the International Court of Justice in The Hague awarded the island to El Salvador in 1992, in preference to claims from Honduras and Nicaragua.

A *lancha* leaves La Unión for the town of **Meanguera del Golfo**, on Meanguera. The journey across the gulf is beautiful, with tranquil waters, fishing boats and views to the surrounding mountains. The island has secluded beaches with good bathing; for example, Majahual (a 45-minute walk), fringed with palm trees. About 2400 people live on this carefree island, where painted boats float in the cove surrounded by small *tiendas* and *comedores* that serve fish, shark and prawns. The highest point on the island is **Cerro de Evaristo** at 512 m. Launches leave La Unión daily at 1000, or private boats may leave earlier when full; the journey takes 45 minutes, US$2-3. It's possible to arrange transport with a local boatman to Coyolito (Honduras), Isla Amapala, or for day trips around the gulf (about US$80), but make sure the price is agreed beforehand. You can travel to Honduras or Nicaragua if you have visited immigration in La Unión first to get the necessary paperwork.

Listings La Unión

Where to stay

$ San Francisco
Calle General Menéndez 6-3, Barrio Concepción, T2604-4159.
Clean and friendly, some rooms with hammocks and fan. Noisy and has some water supply problems, but OK. Safe parking.

Around La Unión

$$$ Hotel Joya del Golfo
Isla de Meanguera, T2648-0072.

Wonderfully relaxing hotel in the next bay beyond the harbour (ask the *lancha* from La Unión to drop you off), run by an extremely hospitable US-Salvadorean family. There are 4 lovely rooms, beautifully furnished, with 4-poster beds, a/c, cable TV and balcony. Excellent food in cosy family lounge, with books, games and DVDs. Kayaks for guests and boat to nearby beaches (US$10), plus hikes around island. Reservations essential. Highly recommended.

$ Hotel Paraíso
Meanguera del Golfo.
Has rooms with TV, private bath and hot water. Recommended.

Restaurants

Bottled water is hard to find, but *agua helada* from clean sources is sold (US$0.25 a bag). There are several cheap *comedores* to choose from; try Comedores Gallego (**$**) and Rosita (**$**), recommended. Comedor Tere (**$**), Av General Menéndez 2.2, is also good.

$$ Amanecer Marino
On the waterfront.
Beautiful view of the bay and good for watching the world go by. Serves seafood.

$ Las Lunas
3 blocks from the central park.
Nice atmosphere. Very popular among locals.

$ Restaurante Puerto Viejo
Located in front of El Dragón.
Big portions, cheap. Best seafood in town; try *tazón de sopa de pescado.*

Transport

Bus The terminal is at 3 Calle Pte (block 3). To **San Salvador**, bus 304, US$2, 2-3 hrs, many daily, direct or via San Miguel, 1 passes the harbour at 0300. Bus 324 to **San Miguel,** US$1. Bus to Honduran border at **El Amatillo**, No 353, US$1.80; see also box, page 112.

Eastern
Pacific coast

As yet unexploited, the Pacific shoreline east of San Salvador does not boast the big resorts and surf enclaves of the west, although it does have the Costa del Sol, the most developed tourist destination in the region. For those willing to get off the beaten track, there are more tranquil and intriguing possibilities, including isolated beaches, teeming mangroves and lagoons filled with marine life. For many travellers, the region presents an adventurous route to the Nicaraguan border and the Gulf of Fonseca, whose cut-off islands present special appeal.

East of La Libertad

remote beaches and tangled mangroves

The road to La Unión runs east through the southern cotton lands. It begins on a four-lane motorway to the airport at Comalapa. The first place of any importance is at Km 13, Santo Tomás where there are pre-Hispanic ruins at Cushululitán, a short distance north. A road to the east, rising to 1000 m, runs south of Lago de Ilopango to join the Pan-American Highway beyond Cojutepeque.

From Santo Tomás it's 10 km on to **Olocuilta**, an old town famed for its church and known worldwide for its rice dough *pupusas*. It hosts a colourful market on Sundays under a great tree. Both Santo Tomás and Olocuilta can be reached by bus 133 from San Salvador. The highway to the airport crosses the Carretera Litoral (CA 2) near the towns of San Luis Talpa and Comalapa. The coastal road goes east, through Rosario de la Paz, across Río Jiboa and on to Zacatecoluca.

Costa del Sol

Just after Rosario, a branch road to the south leads to **La Herradura** (bus 153 from Terminal del Sur to La Herradura, US$1.25, 1½ hours) and the Playa Costa del Sol on the Pacific, which is being developed as a tourist resort. The beach is on a narrow peninsula, along the length of which are private houses which prevent access to the sand until you reach the **Turicentro** ⓘ *0800-1800*. Here, *cabañas* can be rented for the day or for 24 hours, but they are not suitable for sleeping. Playa Costa del Sol is crowded at weekends and holidays, as there are extensive sandy beaches. However, the sea has a mild undertow; so go carefully until you are sure. Expensive hotels are continuously popping up but prices are a bit over the top; budget travellers might choose some of the smaller hotels by Playa Los Blancos. On the road to Costa del Sol, there is also a great water park, **Atlantis Water Park** ⓘ *Km 51, carretera Costa del Sol, T2211-4103, www.atlantis.com.sv, US$10; children US$6, on bus routes No 495 and 143 (every 15 mins).* Options from San Salvador include hotel pickup, small lunch and entrance from US$15-20.

Isla Tasajera

At the southeast end of the Costa del Sol road, near the **Pacific Paradise** hotel, a ferry (US$1.75) leaves for Isla Tasajera in the Estero de Jaltepeque (tidal lagoon). For boat excursions, take the Costa del Sol bus to the last stop at La Puntilla and negotiate with the local boatmen. Boat hire for the day costs US$75, including pilot. It's a great trip into the lagoon, with mangroves, dolphin watching and trips up to the river mouth of the Río Lempa (the longest river in the country).

Zacatecoluca

The capital of La Paz Department is 56 km from San Salvador by road and 19 km south of San Vicente. Zacatecoluca (altitude 201 m, population 65,826) is a good place to buy hammocks (for example nylon 'doubles', US$13). José Simeón Cañas, who abolished slavery in Central America, was born here. There is a cathedral in the Moorish style and an excellent art gallery as well as a mall with a supermarket and several stores.

Ichanmichen

Admission and car parking US$0.75 per person, bungalow rental US$4.

Near the town is the park and Turicentro of Ichanmichen ('the place of the little fish'). It is crossed by canals and decorated with natural spring pools where you can swim. It is very hot but there is plenty of shade.

Usulután, Playa El Espino and Laguna El Jocotal

About 110 km from the capital is Usulután, capital of its department. It's a large, dirty and unsafe place, and only useful as a transit point (bus No 302 from San Salvador, US$1.40). The coastal highway goes direct from Usulután to La Unión.

Playa El Espino can be reached from Usulután, by car (4WD), pickup or slow bus; it is very remote but lovely. Some small hotels and restaurants operate, but most only at weekends. To visit the reserve, enquire at the entrance; hire a boat to see more.

Beyond Usulután, the impressive silhouette of **Volcán Chaparrasque** rises out of the flat coastal plain. Two roads go northeast to San Miguel, the first from 10 km along at El Tránsito, the second a further 5 km east, which keeps to the low ground south and east of Volcán San Miguel. Two kilometres beyond this turning on the Carretera Litoral is a short road to the right leading to Laguna El Jocotal, a national nature reserve supported by the World Wildlife Fund, which has an abundance of birds and snakes.

Playa El Cuco and around
Bus No 320 to San Miguel, US$0.45, 1 hr, last bus 1600.

About 12 km from the junction for San Miguel there is a turning to the right leading in 7 km to Playa El Cuco, a popular beach with several cheap places to stay near the bus station. The main beach is liable to get crowded and dirty at weekends and holidays, but is deserted mid-week. Single women should take care here; locals warn against walking along the beach after sunset. Cases of malaria have been reported. Another popular beach, **El Tamarindo**, is reached by following the coastal road a little further before taking a right turn.

Listings East of La Libertad

Where to stay

Costa del Sol
Cheaper accommodation can be found 1 km east at Playa Los Blancos and in La Herradura.

$$ Izalco Cabaña Club
30 rooms and a pool. Good value, seafood is a speciality.

$ Miny Hotel y Restaurant Mila
Km 66, opposite police station.
Very friendly, owner Marcos speaks English. Clean, simple, fan, pool, good food, beach access. Take bus No 495 from Terminal Sur, San Salvador; buses are very crowded at weekends, but the resort is quiet during the week.

Playa El Cuco and around

$$ Trópico Club
2.5 km along the coast from Playa El Cuco, T2682-1073, tropicoinn@yahoo.com.

Several cabins, pool and open-air dining. Leads directly to the beach. Run by the **Trópico Inn** in San Miguel (T2661-1800); see page 70.

$ Los Leones Marinos
El Cuco, T2619-9015.
Clean and tidy with bath.

Playa Las Flores

$$$$-$$$ Las Flores Surf Resort
Close to Playa El Cuco, T2619-9118, www. lasflores resort.com.
Run by surf expert Rodrigo Barraza, this boutique hotel caters mostly for foreign tourists, making an excellent choice for an upscale budget.

Playa Torola

$$ Torola Cabaña Club
Km 175, T2681-5528.
This friendly place with a welcoming owner has a pool looking out to sea and a great open-air bar/restaurant. Recommended.

Restaurants

Costa del Sol

$ Restaurante Kenny Mar
Km 60, Cra Costa del Sol, Playa San
Marcelino, T2338-2578.
Delicious seafood with beachfront view.

Transport

Zacatecoluca
Bus No 133 from Terminal Sur, **San Salvador**. Direct bus to **La Libertad** 1540 (US$0.85), or take San Salvador bus, change at Comalapa, 2 hrs.

Playa El Cuco and around
Boat Boat from El Tamarindo across the bay leads to a short cut to **La Unión**.

Bus From **La Unión**, 20 mins.

Background
El Salvador

Regional history

Arrival of the American people

While controversy continues to surround the precise date humans arrived in the Americas, the current prevailing view suggests the first wave of emigrants travelled between Siberia and Alaska across the Bering Strait ice bridge created in the last Ice Age, approximately 15,000 years ago. Small hunter-gatherer groups quickly moved through the region, and in fertile lands they developed agriculture and settled. By 1500 BC sedentary villages were widespread in many parts of the Americas, including Central America, where stone-built cities and complex civilizations also began to emerge.

Pre-Columbian civilizations

Despite the wide variety of climates and terrains that fall within Central America's boundaries, the so-called Mesoamerican civilizations were interdependent, sharing the same agriculture based on maize, beans and squash, as well as many sociological traits. These included an enormous pantheon of gods, pyramid-building, a trade in valuable objects, hieroglyphic writing, astronomy, mathematics and a complex calendar system. Historians divide Mesoamerican civilizations into three broad periods, the **pre-Classic**, which lasted until about AD 300, the **Classic**, until AD 900, and the **post-Classic**, from AD 900 until the Spanish conquest.

Olmecs

Who precisely the Olmecs were, where they came from and why they disappeared is a matter of debate. It is known that they flourished from about **1400-400 BC**, lived in the **Mexican Gulf coast** region between Veracruz and Tabasco, and that all later civilizations have their roots in Olmec culture. They are particularly renowned for their carved **colossal heads**, jade figures and altar. They gave great importance to the jaguar and the serpent in their imagery and built large ceremonial centres such as **San Lorenzo** and **La Venta**. The progression from the Olmec to the Maya civilization seems to have taken place at Izapa on the Pacific border of present-day Mexico and Guatemala.

Maya

The best known of the pre-Conquest civilizations were the Maya, thought to have evolved in a formative period in the **Pacific highlands** of Guatemala and El Salvador between **1500 BC** and about **AD 100**. After 200 years of growth it entered what is known today as its Classic period, when the civilization flourished in Guatemala, El Salvador, Belize, Honduras and southern Mexico. The height of the Classic period lasted until AD 900, after which the Maya resettled in the Yucatán, possibly after a devastating famine, drought or peasant uprising. They then came under the influence of the central Mexican Toltecs, who were highly militaristic, until the Spanish conquest in the 16th century.

Throughout its evolution, Mayan civilization was based on independent city states that were governed by a theocratic elite of priests, nobles and warriors. Recent research has revealed that these cities, far from being the peaceful ceremonial centres once imagined, were **warring adversaries** striving to capture victims for sacrifice. This change in perception of the Maya was largely due to a greater understanding of Mayan **hieroglyphic writing**, which appears both on paper codices and on stone monuments. Aside from a gory preoccupation with sacrifice, Mayan culture was rich in **ceremony**, **art**, **science**, **folklore** and **dance**. Their cities were all meticulously designed according to strict and highly symbolic geometric rules: columns, figures, faces, animals, friezes, stairways and temples often expressed a date, a time or a specific astronomical relationship. Impressively, the Mayan calendar was so advanced that it was a nearer approximation to sidereal time than either the Julian or the Gregorian calendars of Europe; it was only .000069 of a day out of true in a year. The Maya also formulated the concept of 'zero' centuries in advance of the Old World, plotted the movements of the sun, moon, Venus and other planets, and conceived a time cycle of more than 1800 million days.

Conquest

It was only during his fourth voyage, in 1502, that **Columbus** reached the mainland of Central America. He landed in **Costa Rica** and Panama, which he called **Veragua**, and founded the town of Santa María de Belén. In 1508 Alonso de Ojeda received a grant of land on the Pearl coast east of Panama, and in 1509 he founded the town of San Sebastián, later moved to a new site called Santa María la Antigua del Darién (now in Colombia). In 1513 the governor of the colony at Darién was **Vasco Núñez de Balboa**. Taking 190 men he crossed the isthmus in 18 days and caught the first glimpse of the Pacific; he claimed it and all neighbouring lands in the name of the King of Spain. But from the following year, when **Pedrarias de Avila** replaced him as Governor, Núñez de Balboa fell on evil days, and he was executed by Pedrarias in 1519. That same year Pedrarias crossed the isthmus and founded the town of Panamá on the Pacific side. It was in April 1519, too, that **Cortés** began his conquest of Mexico. Central America was explored from these two nodal points of Panama and Mexico.

Settlement

The groups of Spanish settlers were few and widely scattered, a fundamental point in explaining the **political fragmentation** of Central America today. Panama was ruled from Bogotá, but the rest of Central America was subordinate to the Viceroyalty at Mexico City, with Antigua, Guatemala, as an Audiencia for the area until 1773, and thereafter Guatemala City. Panama was of paramount importance for colonial Spanish America for its strategic position, and for the trade passing across the isthmus to and from the southern colonies. The other provinces were of comparatively little value.

The small number of **Spaniards intermarried** freely with the locals, accounting for the predominance of mestizos in present-day Central America. But the picture has regional variations. In Guatemala, where there was the highest native population density, intermarriage affected fewer of the natives, and over half the population today is still purely *indígena* (**indigenous**). On the Meseta Central of Costa Rica, the natives were all but wiped out by disease and, as a consequence of this great disaster, there is a community of over two million whites, with little *indígena* admixture. **Blacks** predominate along the Caribbean coast of Central America. Most were brought in as cheap labour to work as railway builders and banana planters in the 19th century and canal cutters in the 20th. The **Garífuna** people, living between southern Belize and Nicaragua, arrived in the area as free people after African slaves and indigenous Caribbean people intermingled following a shipwreck off St Vincent.

Independence and after

On 5 November 1811, **José Matías Delgado**, a priest and jurist born in San Salvador, organized a revolt with another priest, Manuel José Arce. They proclaimed the Independence of El Salvador, but the Audiencia at Guatemala City suppressed the revolt and took Delgado prisoner. Eleven years later, in 1820, the revolution of Spain itself precipitated the Independence of Central America. On 24 February 1821, the Mexican **General Agustín de Iturbide** announced his **Plan de Iguala** for an independent Mexico. Several months later, the Central American *criollos* followed his example and announced their own **Declaration of Independence** in Guatemala City on 15 September 1821. Iturbide invited the provinces of Central America to join with him and, on 5 January 1822, Central America was annexed to Mexico. Delgado, however, refused to accept this decree and Iturbide, who had now assumed the title of **Emperor Agustín I**, sent an army south under Vicente Filísola to enforce it. Filísola had completed his task when he heard of Iturbide's abdication, and at once convened a general congress of the Central American provinces. It met on 24 June 1823, and thereafter established the **Provincias Unidas del Centro de América**. The Mexican Republic acknowledged their Independence on 1 August 1824, and Filísola's soldiers were withdrawn.

The United Provinces of Central America

In 1824, the first congress, presided over by Delgado, appointed a provisional governing *junta* which promulgated a constitution modelled on that of the United States. The Province of Chiapas was not included in the Federation, as it had already adhered to Mexico in 1821. Guatemala City, by force of tradition, soon became the seat of government.

The first president under the new constitution was **Manuel José Arce**, a liberal. One of his first acts was to **abolish slavery**. El Salvador, protesting that he had exceeded his powers, rose in December 1826. Honduras, Nicaragua and Costa Rica joined the revolt, and in 1828 **General Francisco Morazán**, in charge of the army of Honduras, defeated the federal forces, entered San Salvador and marched against Guatemala City. He captured the city on 13 April 1829, and established that contradiction in terms: a liberal dictatorship. Many conservative leaders were expelled and church and monastic properties confiscated. Morazán himself became President of the Federation in 1830. He was a man of considerable ability; he ruled with a strong hand, encouraged education, fostered trade and industry, opened the country to immigrants, and reorganized the administration. In 1835 the capital was moved to San Salvador.

These reforms antagonized the conservatives and there were several uprisings. The most serious revolt was among the *indígenas* of Guatemala, led by Rafael Carrera, an illiterate mestizo conservative and a born leader. Years of continuous warfare followed, during the course of which the Federation withered away. As a result, the federal congress passed an act which allowed each province to assume the government it chose, but the idea of a federation was not quite dead. Morazán became President of El Salvador. Carrera, who was by then in control of Guatemala, defeated Morazán in battle and forced him to leave the country. But in 1842, Morazán overthrew Braulio Carrillo, then dictator of Costa Rica, and became president himself. At once he set about rebuilding the Federation, but a popular uprising soon led to his capture. He was shot on 15 September 1842 and with him perished any practical hope of Central American political union.

The separate states

The history of **Guatemala**, **El Salvador**, **Honduras** and **Nicaragua** since the breakdown of federation has been tempestuous in the extreme (**Costa Rica**, with its mainly white population and limited economic value at the time, is a country apart, and **Panama** was Colombian territory until 1903). In each, the ruling class was divided into pro-clerical conservatives and anti-clerical liberals, with constant changes of power. Each was weak, and tried repeatedly to buttress its weakness by alliances with others, which invariably broke up because one of the allies sought a position of mastery. The wars were mainly ideological wars between conservatives and liberals, or wars motivated by inflamed nationalism. Nicaragua was riven internally by the mutual hatreds of the Conservatives of Granada and the Liberals of León, and there were repeated conflicts between the Caribbean and interior parts of Honduras. Despite the permutations and combinations of external and civil war there has been a recurrent desire to re-establish some form of **La Gran Patria Centroamericana**. Throughout the 19th century, and far into the 20th, there have been ambitious projects for political federation, usually involving El Salvador, Honduras and Nicaragua; none of them lasted more than a few years.

Regional integration

Poverty, the fate of the great majority, has brought about closer economic cooperation between the five republics, and in 1960 they established the **Central American Common Market** (CACM). Surprisingly, the Common Market appeared to be a great success until 1968, when integration fostered national antagonisms, and there was a growing conviction in Honduras and Nicaragua, which were doing least well out of integration, that they were being exploited by the others. In 1969 the Football War broke out between El Salvador and Honduras, basically because of a dispute about illicit emigration by Salvadoreans into Honduras, and relations between the two were not normalized until 1980. Hopes for improvement were revived in 1987 when the Central American Peace Plan, drawn up by President Oscar Arias Sánchez of Costa Rica, was signed by the presidents of Guatemala, El Salvador, Honduras, Nicaragua and Costa Rica. The plan proposed formulae to end the civil strife in individual countries, achieving this aim first in Nicaragua (1989), then in El Salvador (1991). In Guatemala, a ceasefire after 36 years of war led to the signing of a peace accord at the end of 1996. With the signing of peace accords, emphasis has shifted to regional, economic and environmental integration.

In October 1993, the presidents of Guatemala, El Salvador, Honduras, Nicaragua and Costa Rica signed a new **Central American Integration Treaty Protocol** to replace that of 1960 and set up new mechanisms for regional integration. The Treaty was the culmination of a series of annual presidential summits held since 1986 which, besides aiming for peace and economic integration, established a Central American Parliament and a Central American Court of Justice. Attempts at further economic and regional integration continue. Plans to create a **Free Trade Area of the Americas** (FTAA) appear to have failed, but the 2003 **Dominican Republic-Central American Free Trade Agreement** (DR-CAFTA) has now been signed by several nations including the Dominican Republic, Guatemala, El Salvador, Honduras, Nicaragua and Costa Rica.

The DR-CAFTA closely compliments the 2001 **Plan Puebla-Panama** (the PPP, also known as the Mesoamerican Integration and Development Project) an economic corridor stretching from Puebla, west of Mexico City, as far as Panama. Supporters of the plan see it as a means for economic development. Critics see it as a way of draining cheap labour and natural resources with little concern for the environment or long-term progress. Today, the PPP simmers on the back burner, but the desire for Central American nations to strengthen ties is regularly voiced. This is most apparent in the creation of Central America 4 (CA-4), a 2006 border control agreement between Guatemala, El Salvador, Honduras and Nicaragua, that opens up travel between the four nations. Regional meetings occur periodically to promote and encourage trust and cooperation, and while the final destination of such cooperation is far from clear, the Central America of today is far more productive and safer than it was in the 1980s and early 1990s.

El Salvador

History

When Spanish expeditions arrived in El Salvador from Guatemala and Nicaragua, they found it quite densely populated by several indigenous groups, of whom the most populous were the **Pipiles**. By 1550, the Spaniards had occupied the country, many living in existing indigenous villages and towns. The settlers cultivated cocoa in the volcanic highlands and balsam along the coast, and introduced cattle to roam the grasslands freely. Towards the end of the 16th century, indigo became the big export crop: production was controlled by the Spaniards, and the indigenous population provided the workforce, many suffering illness as a result. A period of regional turmoil accompanied El Salvador's declaration of Independence from the newly autonomous political body of Central America in 1839: indigenous attempts to regain their traditional land rights were put down by force.

Coffee emerged as an important cash crop in the second half of the 19th century, bringing with it improvements in transport facilities and the final abolition of indigenous communal lands.

The land question was a fundamental cause of the peasant uprising of 1932, which was brutally crushed by the dictator **General Maximiliano Hernández Martínez**. Following his overthrow in 1944, the military did not relinquish power: a series of military coups kept them in control, while they protected the interests of the landowning oligarchy.

1980s Civil War

The most recent military coup, in October 1979, led to the formation of a civilian-military junta which promised far-reaching reforms. When these were not carried out, the opposition unified forming a broad coalition, the Frente Democrático Revolucionario, which adopted a military wing, the **Farabundo Martí National Liberation Front (FMLN)** in 1980. Later the same year, the Christian Democrat **Ingeniero José Napoleón Duarte** was named as President of the Junta. At about the same time, political tension reached the proportions of civil war.

Duarte was elected to the post of president in 1984, following a short administration headed by Dr Alvaro Magaña. Duarte's periods of power were characterized by a partly successful attempt at land reform, the nationalization of foreign trade and the banking system, and violence. In addition to deaths in combat, 40,000 civilians were killed between 1979 and 1984, mostly by right-wing death squads. Among the casualties was **Archbishop Oscar Romero**, who was shot while saying mass in March 1980. Nothing came of meetings between Duarte's government and the FMLN, which were aimed at seeking a peace agreement. The war continued in stalemate until 1989, by which time an estimated 70,000 had been killed. The Christian Democrats' inability to end the war, reverse the economic decline or rebuild after the 1986 earthquake, combined with their reputation for corruption, brought about a resurgence of support for the right-wing National Republican Alliance (ARENA). An FMLN offer to participate in presidential elections, dependent on certain conditions, was not accepted and the ARENA candidate, **Alfredo Cristiani**, won the presidency comfortably in March 1989, taking office in June. Peace talks again failed to produce results and in November 1989 the FMLN guerrillas staged their most ambitious offensive ever, which paralysed the capital and caused a violent backlash from government forces. FMLN-government negotiations resumed with UN mediation following the offensive, but the two sides could not reach agreement about the purging of the armed forces, which had become the most wealthy institution in the country following 10 years of US support.

Peace negotiations

Although El Salvador's most left-wing political party, the Unión Democrática Nacionalista, agreed to participate in municipal elections in 1991, the FMLN remained outside the electoral process, and the civil war continued unresolved. Talks were held in Venezuela and Mexico after initial agreement was reached in April on reforms to the electoral and judicial systems, but further progress was stalled over the restructuring of the armed forces and disarming the guerrillas. There were hopes that human rights would improve after the establishment in June 1991 of a UN Security Council human rights observer commission (ONUSAL), which was charged with verifying compliance with the human rights agreement signed by the Government and the FMLN in Geneva in April 1990. Finally, after considerable UN assistance, the FMLN and the Government signed a peace accord in New York in January 1992 and a formal ceasefire began the following month. A detailed schedule throughout 1992 was established to demobilize the FMLN, dismantle five armed forces elite battalions and to initiate land requests by ex-combatants from both sides. The demobilization process was reported as completed in December 1992, formally concluding the civil war. The US agreed at this point to 'forgive' a substantial portion of the US$2 billion international debt of El Salvador. In March 1993, the United Nations Truth Commission published its investigation of human rights abuses during the civil war. Five days later, the legislature approved a general amnesty for all those involved in criminal activities in the war. This included those named in the Truth Commission report. The Cristiani government was slow to implement not only the constitutional reforms proposed by the Truth Commission, but also the process of land reform and the establishment of the National Civilian Police (PNC). By 1995, when Cristiani's successor had taken office, the old national police force was demobilized, but the PNC suffered from a lack of resources for its proper establishment. In fact, the budget for the implementation of the final peace accords was inadequate and El Salvador had to ask the UN for financial assistance.

1994 elections and after

Presidential and congressional elections in 1994 failed to give an outright majority to any presidential candidate and **Calderón Sol** of ARENA won the run-off election.

Besides his government's difficulties with the final stages of the peace accord, his first months in office were marked by rises in the cost of living, increases in crime, strikes and protests, and occupations of the Legislature by ex-combatants. Frustration at the slow rate of reform came in the form of criticism from the United Nations and in March 1997 through the ballot box. Only 41% of the electorate bothered to vote. In the National Assembly, Arena won 29 seats, narrowly beating the FMLN which increased its tally to 28 seats. The National Conciliation Party (PCN) won 11, the Christian Democrats (PDC) nine and minority parties seven seats. FMLN managed to run neck-and-neck with Arena until within a year of the March 1999 presidential elections. The party's inability to select a presidential candidate, however, caused it to lose ground rapidly. Arena's candidate, **Fransisco Flores**, won the election but still with a poor turn-out of less than 40% of the electorate. In the face of such a huge rejection of the political system Flores could not claim a clear mandate. Most interpreted the abstention as a lack of faith in any party's ability to solve the twin problems of poverty and crime. Elections in March 2004 won a five-year term for **Tony Saca**, the fourth successive victory for the right-wing Arena party. The former radio and TV presenter promised to crack down on criminal gangs and promote ties with the US.

Into the 21st century

If the devastating earthquakes of early 2001 were not enough for the country to deal with, droughts through the summer months led to a food crisis that required United Nations' intervention. Old rivalries flared briefly as Honduras expelled two Salvadorean diplomats on spying charges, displaying the fragility of the cordial relations with the northern neighbour. El Salvador also hosted the meeting of Mexican and Central America presidents to develop the controversial **Plan Puebla-Panama** regional integration project which would link the Mexican city of Puebla with Panama City along an economic investment corridor. In 2002, promising signs of progress and support for the future led US President Bush to call El Salvador one of the "really bright lights" in the region.

The country's lively landscape continued to shape events with the eruption of Ilamatepec volcano, also known as Santa Ana, in October 2005, quickly followed by the destructive floods and mudslides of Hurricane Stan which killed over 70 people, and forced over 36,000 to seek refuge in emergency shelters. In 2006 El Salvador continued to lead the way for regional integration as the first country to fully implement the Central American Free Trade Agreement with the US. The regional confidence continued and El Salvador and Honduras inaugurated their newly defined border in April 2006, bringing to an end the dispute that led to the outbreak of war between the two nations in 1969. In March 2011, the Inter-American Commission on Human Rights prepared to reopen the court case investigating the massacre of some 1000 civilians in village of El Mozote in December 1981, the bloodiest episode in the country's civil war. In the same month, US President Barack Obama offered US$200m to help El Salvador fight drug traffickers and gang violence. The money is part of the $1.5bn 'Mérida Initiative' announced in 2007 to combat the drugs cartels. Critics say that the US military aid deployed to

Central America is contributing to the region's re-militarization, which may have more to do with securing resources for exploitation than with stopping the flow of cocaine.

In 2014, presidential elections were narrowly won by Salvador Sánchez Cerén of the left-wing Farabundo Martí National Liberation Front, a figure very much moulded by his experiences within revolutionary organizations.

Culture

People

The population of 6.7 million people is far more homogeneous than that of Guatemala. The reason for this is that El Salvador lay comparatively isolated from the main stream of conquest, and had no precious metals to act as magnets for the Spaniards. The small number of Spanish settlers intermarried with those indigenous locals who survived the plagues brought from Europe to form a group of mestizos. There were only about half a million people as late as 1879. With the introduction of coffee, the population grew quickly and the new prosperity fertilized the whole economy, but the internal pressure of population has led to the occupation of all the available land. Several hundred thousand Salvadoreans have emigrated to neighbouring republics because of the shortage of land and the concentration of land ownership, and, more recently, because of the civil war.

Of the total population, some 10% are regarded as ethnic indigenous, although the traditional indigenous culture has almost completely vanished. Other estimates put the percentage of the pure indigenous population as low as 5%. The Lenca and the Pipil, the two surviving indigenous groups, are predominantly peasant farmers. Only 1% are of unmixed white ancestry, the rest are mestizos.

With a population of 322 to the square kilometre, El Salvador is the most densely populated country on the American mainland. Health and sanitation outside the capital and some of the main towns leave much to be desired.

Music and dance

The Mexican music industry seems to exert an overwhelming cultural influence, while the virtual absence of an indigenous population may also be partly responsible, since it is so often they who maintain traditions and connections with the past. Whatever the reason, the visitor who is seeking specifically Salvadorean native music will find little to satisfy him or her. El Salvador is an extension of 'marimba country', but songs and dances are often accompanied by the guitar and seem to lack a rhythm or style that can be pinpointed as specifically local. An exception is the music played on the *pito de caña* and *tambor* which accompanies the traditional dances called *Danza de los Historiantes*, *La Historia* or *Los Moros y Cristianos*. Over 30 types of dance have been identified, mostly in the west and centre of the country, although there are a few in the east. The main theme is the conflict between christianized and 'heretic' *indígenas* and the dances are performed as a ritual on the local saint's day.

Education and religion

State education is free and nominally obligatory. There are 43 universities, three national and the others private or church-affiliated. There is also a National School of Agriculture. The most famous are the government-financed Universidad Nacional and the Jesuit-run Universidad Centroamericana. Roman Catholicism is the prevailing religion.

Land and environment

El Salvador is the smallest, most densely populated and most integrated of the Central American republics. Its intermont basins are a good deal lower than those of Guatemala, rising to little more than 600 m at the capital, San Salvador. Across this upland and surmounting it run two more or less parallel rows of volcanoes, 14% of which are over 900 m high. The highest are Santa Ana (2365 m), San Vicente (2182 m), San Miguel (2130 m), and San Salvador (1893 m). One important result of this volcanic activity is that the highlands are covered with a deep layer of ash and lava which forms a porous soil ideal for coffee planting.

The total area of El Salvador is 21,000 sq km. Guatemala is to the west, Honduras to the north and east, and the Pacific coastline to the south is approximately 321 km long. Lowlands lie to the north and south of the high backbone. In the south, on the Pacific coast, the lowlands of Guatemala are confined to just east of Acajutla; beyond are lava promontories before another 30-km belt of lowlands where the 325-km long Río Lempa flows into the sea. The northern lowlands are in the wide depression along the course of the Río Lempa, buttressed to the south by the highlands of El Salvador and to the north by the basalt cliffs edging the highlands of Honduras. The highest point in El Salvador, Cerro El Pital (2730 m) is part of the mountain range bordering on Honduras. After 160 km the Lempa cuts through the southern uplands to reach the Pacific; the depression is prolonged southeast till it reaches the Gulf of Fonseca.

El Salvador is located on the southwest coast of the Central American Isthmus on the Pacific Ocean. As the only country in the region lacking access to the Caribbean Sea, it does not possess the flora associated with that particular coastal zone. El Salvador nevertheless has a wide variety of colourful, tropical vegetation; for example over 200 species of orchid grow all over the country. As a result of excessive forest cutting, and hence the destruction of their habitats, many of the animals (such as jaguars and crested eagles) once found in the highlands of the country, have diminished at an alarming rate. In response to this problem several nature reserves have been set up in areas where flora and fauna can be found in their most unspoilt state. Among these nature reserves are the Cerro Verde, Deininger Park, El Imposible Woods, El Jocatal Lagoon and the Montecristo Cloudforest.

Practicalities
El Salvador

Getting there

Air

From Europe To Miami with any transatlantic carrier, then to San Salvador with **American Airlines** or **Taca. Iberia** flies from Barcelona and Madrid via Miami.

The international airport is at Comalapa, 62 km southeast of San Salvador off the Coastal Highway, reached by a four-lane toll highway. There is a tourist information desk at the airport, which is open sporadically. If closed, you can still pick up some useful leaflets. Taxis and buses provide regular links to the capital. See also page 36.

There is a 13% tax on international air tickets bought in El Salvador and an airport departure tax of US\$32 for anyone staying more than six hours. The airport departure tax is now included in the ticket. The phone number for the airport authorities (**CEPA**) is T2339-9455. The airport has offices for all the main car rental companies and there are two banks, a tourist office and **Grupo Taca** and **American Airline** offices. Border formalities tend to be relatively brief although searches may be carried out.

From USA and Canada The main connection is with Miami. Other cities with flights to San Salvador are Atlanta, Dallas/Fort Worth, Houston, Los Angeles, Montreal, New Orleans, New York, Orlando, Phoenix, San Diego, San Francisco, Washington and Toronto.

From Central America and Mexico There are flights from all capitals and many larger cities in Mexico.

From South America There are good connections to Colombia with a few flights to Barranquilla and Bogotá. Flights also operate to Buenos Aires, Cali, Caracas, Cartagena, Cucutá, Guayaquil, Quito, Lima, Medellín, Santa Marta and Santiago. Some flights go via San José or Panama City.

Road

There are several border crossings with neighbouring countries. To the west the Pan-American Highway arrives from Guatemala at San Cristóbal through Santa Ana, Las Chinamas and La Hachadura, which is handy for Parque Nacional El Imposible. To the northwest the crossing is at Anguiatú. Also to the northwest the crossing at El Poy leads to southern Honduras, as does the crossing to the northeast at Perquín and to the east at El Amatillo. See also boxes, pages 111, 112 and 113. For border crossing phone numbers, see Customs and duty free, page 114.

Getting around

Road

Bus

Bus services are good and cover most areas, although the buses are usually crowded. The best time to travel by bus is 0900-1500; avoid Friday and Sunday afternoons. All bus routes have a number, some also have a letter. Strange as it may seem, the system works and the route numbers don't change. Tickets are still unbelievably cheap, both within cities – usually around US$0.25 – and for long-distance journeys, which rarely cost more than US$1.50. Buses are brightly painted, particularly around San Miguel.

Transport is not difficult for budget travellers as nearly all buses have luggage racks inside. For bigger bags there is sometimes space at the back where a couple of seats have been removed, so sit near there if you want to stay close to your bag. However, when problems on buses do occur they are usually at the back of the bus. The cheaper alternatives to the Pullman buses, which cross to Guatemala and Tegucigalpa from Puerto Bus Terminal in San Salvador, have luggage compartments beneath them and the luggage is tagged.

Car

At the border, after producing a driving licence and proof of ownership, you are given a *comprobante de ingreso* (which has to be stamped by immigration, customs and quarantine); this is free of charge and you get the vehicle permit for 60 days. You need to have a passport from the same country as your driving licence or have an international licence and not have been in the country for more than 60 days. (If you are a foreigner residing in El Salvador you need to get a Salvadorean driver's licence.) You receive a receipt, vehicle permit and vehicle check document. Under no circumstances may the 60 days be extended, even though the driver may have been granted 90 days in the country. A few kilometres

---

TRAVEL TIP

Border cooperation

In June 2006, Guatemala, El Salvador, Honduras, and Nicaragua entered into a 'Central America-4 (CA-4) Border Control Agreement'. Under the terms of the agreement, citizens of the four countries may travel freely across land borders from one of the countries to any of the others without completing entry and exit formalities at immigration checkpoints. US citizens and other eligible foreign nationals, who legally enter any of the four countries, may similarly travel among the four without obtaining additional visas or tourist entry permits for the other three countries. Immigration officials at the first port of entry determine the length of stay, up to a maximum period of 90 days.

BORDER CROSSING
El Salvador–Guatemala

El Salvador and Guatemala are covered under the CA-4 border control agreement (see box, opposite), but you must still submit to immigration formalities before proceeding.

San Cristóbal–Frontera

The main Pan-American highway crossing, used by international buses and heavy traffic. Immigration on both sides is open 0600-2200, but it's usually possible to cross outside these hours with extra charges. On the El Salvador side, there are regular buses to Santa Ana, No 201, with connections to San Salvador, 1½ hours. In Guatemala, there are buses to Guatemala City, two to three hours. **Note** Travelling during the hours of darkness is not recommended.

Las Chinamas–Valle Nuevo

The fastest road link from San Salvador to Guatemala City, but it's busy. Change currency with the women in front of the ex-ITSU office. There's a good quetzal-dollar rate. Immigration offices on both sides is open 0800-1800; it's a quick service if your papers are ready. In El Salvador there are frequent buses to Ahuachapán, No 265, 25 minutes, with connecting services to San Salvador, No 202. Alternatively, try to negotiate a seat with an international Pullman bus; most pass between 0800 and 1400. Onwards to Guatemala there are connections to Guatemala City, two hours.

La Hachadura–Ciudad Pedro Alvarado

This border is at the bridge over the Río Paz, with a filling station and a few shops nearby. It's increasingly popular, thanks to improved roads. Private vehicles require a lot of paperwork and can take two hours to process. In El Salvador there's access to El Salvador's Pacific Coast, and there are services to San Salvador's Terminal Occidente, No 498, three hours There are also services to Ahuachapán, No 503, one hour. The last bus to Sonsonate leaves at 1800. Onward to Guatemala, there's access to the Pacific coast and Guatemala City.

Anguiatú

This is normally a quiet border crossing, except when there are special events at Esquipulas in Guatemala. Immigration on both sides is open 0600-1900 and is a relaxed process. Onwards to El Salvador there are buses to Santa Ana, No 235A, two hours. There are also services to Metapán, 40 minutes, from where a rough but very scenic road runs to El Poy. To Guatemala, this crossing has the best highway access if you're heading north to Tikal. Head for the Padre Miguel junction, 19 km from the border, from where you can make connections to Chiquimula and Esquipulas.

BORDER CROSSING

El Salvador–Honduras

El Salvador and Guatemala are covered under the CA-4 border control agreement (see box, page 110), but you must still submit to immigration formalities before proceeding.

El Poy

This crossing between northern El Salvador and southwestern Honduras is straightforward, but it's better to arrive early if you have a long journey ahead. If changing currency, bargain hard with the money-changers. Travelling onwards to Honduras, shuttles carry passengers to Nueva Ocotopeque, 15-20 minutes, where you can catch highway connections north to Santa Rosa de Copán. On the El Salvador side, buses to San Salvador depart hourly, three to four hours, passing La Palma en route, 30 minutes.

El Amatillo

The Río Goascarán forms the border at El Amatillo. If driving, you will be hounded by *tramitadores*, some of them are unethical, but their services aren't really required here anyway. Expect thorough car searches. Both Salvadorean and Honduran immigration are open 0600-1700 with a break for lunch. In Honduras, there are hourly services to Tegucigalpa, four hours; and to Choluteca, every 30 minutes, three hours. In El Salvador, there are regular bus services (No 330) to San Miguel, 1½ hours.

Perquín–Sabanetas

The international boundary here has been variously disputed throughout history. A treaty resolved the disagreement in 2006 and the border now lies 3 km north of Perquín in El Salvador, though it may be impassable after heavy rains. Travel early morning for the best chance of transport connections. There is a Honduran immigration office 5 km inside the country. Note that this is not a major crossing and motorists with international plates are being turned away. Irregular onward bus services go to Marcala in Honduras and San Miguel in El Salvador.

---

from the border the *comprobante* will be checked. When you leave the country a *comprobante de ingreso* must be stamped again and, if you don't intend to return, your permit must be surrendered. Do not overstay your permitted time unless you wish to be fined. Leaving the country for a few days in order to return for a new permit is not recommended as customs officials are wise to this and may fine you anyway. To bring a vehicle in permanently involves a complex procedure costing thousands of dollars.

Petrol costs per US gallon US$3.60 (super), US$3.20 (regular), US$2.80 (diesel), though as everywhere, prices are constantly rising. All fuel is unleaded. **Roads** are very good throughout the country, but look out for crops being dried at the

BORDER CROSSING
El Salvador–Nicaragua

El Salvador and Nicaragua are covered under the CA-4 border control agreement (see box, page 110), but you must still submit to immigration formalities before proceeding.

La Unión–Potosí
Tour operators have begun ferrying tourists across the Gulf of Fonseca (two to three times a week, US$65, but you should also allow up to two hours for formalities) between La Union and Potosí with onward connections to León and San Salvador. Try Cruce del Golfo, www.crucedelgolfo.com. Note the route is much more expensive than going overland, but not necessarily faster. You may get a cheaper deal by gathering a group and negotiating with local boatmen (US$60-100), but check the vessel is seaworthy and includes life jackets.

Salvadorean immigration is open 0600-2200 and Nicaraguan immigration 0800-1600, but is closed for lunch. Onward transport in Nicaragua includes onward buses to Chinandega, three hours, but tour operators can include shuttles with your passage. In El Salvador, there is a bus to San Salvador every 30 minutes. There are also regular buses to the beaches and San Miguel.

roadside or in central reservations. Take care of buses, which travel very fast. Third-party **insurance** is compulsory in El Salvador and can be arranged at the border (enquire first at consulates). Under the 1996 law, **seat belts** must be worn; the fine for not doing so is US$57. The fine for **drink driving** is US$57. If your alcohol level is very high you go straight to jail and have to await the sentence. Do not attempt to bribe the officials. For more information, call **Ministerio de Transporte** ⓘ *T2281-0678 0679*.

Taxi
Apart from in the major cities taxis are rare, especially after dark. However, if you're eating out at night, you can usually arrange a lift at your hotel or restaurant for a small tip.

Essentials A-Z

Accident and emergency

Police: 911; **Fire service**: T2527-7300; **Red Cross**: T2222-5155; **Hospitals**: T2225-4481; **Public hospital**: Rosales T2231-9200.

Customs and duty free

All personal luggage is allowed in free. Also permitted: 50 cigars or 200 cigarettes, and 2 litres of liquor, 2 used cameras or a video recorder, 1 personal stereo, 1 portable computer and new goods up to US$1000 in value (best to have receipts). No restrictions on the import of foreign currency; up to the amount imported and declared may also be exported. Check with www.aduana. gob.sv for full information.

Phone numbers for Salvadorean border crossings: **Hachadura**: T2420-3767, Chinamas: T2401-3601; **San Cristóbal**: T2441-8109; **El Poy**: T2335-9401; **Angiatú**: T2401-0231; **Amatillo**: T2649-9388.

Electricity

110 volts, 60 cycles, AC (US-style flat-pin plugs). Supply is far from stable; important electrical equipment should have surge protectors.

Embassies and consulates

For all El Salvadoran embassies and consulates abroad and for all foreign embassies and consulates in El Salvador, see http://embassy.goabroad.com.

Health

Gastroenteritic diseases are most common. Visitors should take care over what they eat during the first few weeks, and should drink *agua cristal* (purified bottled water). The bags of water sold in the street are not always safe and taste somewhat of rubber. Cases of dengue are rare in adults. For diarrhoea, mild dysentery, amoebas and parasitic infections get *Nodik* tablets from any chemist or large supermarket, approx US$14 for a 3-day cure. El Salvador has one of the best health systems in Central America, so the capital is a good place to sort out problems. You can get a stool sample taken at the **Pro-Familia Hospital**, 25 Av Norte, near Metro Centro, which gives you the result in about 6-12 hrs.

Internet

Internet cafés are widespread in the capital and are now commonplace in smaller places outside San Salvador. Most hotels will offer both internet service and Wi-Fi.

Language

Spanish is the official language and English is widely understood in business and travel industry-related circles.

Media

Newspapers in San Salvador include *Diario de Hoy* (right wing), www. elsalvador.com, and *La Prensa Gráfica* (centre) every morning including Sun, www.laprensagrafica.com; both have the most complete listings of cultural events in San Salvador. *Co Latino* is a left-wing newspaper. *El Mundo* in the afternoons except Sun. US newspapers and magazines are available at leading hotels.

Of the 80 **radio stations**, one is government owned and several are owned by churches.

There are 4 commercial **television stations**, all with national coverage, and 1 government-run station with 2 channels. There are several cable channels, all with CNN news, etc. Most hotels and many guesthouses in San Salvador have cable.

Money US$1=8.75 colones (fixed).

El Salvador adopted the dollar on 1 Jan 2001 and the national currency the colón is now totally replaced. All US coinage and notes are widely used, although you may have problems with US$20 bills and above. There are some small shops and street merchants that still price their products in colones, but they are in the minority.

ATMs and exchange

Credit cards are widely accepted and are charged at the official rate. You can use credit cards in pretty much any store (except small *tiendas*). Do not find yourself in the countryside without cash or credit cards. There are international Visa and MasterCard ATMs in El Salvador and larger cities throughout the country. For cash advances on Visa or MasterCard, go to **Aval-Visa** or **Banco de América Central de El Salvador**. All ATMs and banks give US dollars in cash (so no need for exchange). Pretty much all gas stations have ATMs.

If you don't want to carry lots of cash, prepaid currency cards allow you to preload money from your bank account, fixed at the day's exchange rate. They look like a credit or debit card and are issued by specialist money-changing companies, such as **Travelex** and **Caxton FX**, and the **Post Office**. You can top up and check your balance by phone, online and sometimes by text.

Traveller's cheques (TCs) are of limited use outside the capital and major cities. Be aware that some banks will want to see your original purchase receipt.

Cost of living and travelling

El Salvador is reasonably priced and 2 people should be able to travel for US$40 per person per day. However, the range of services open to foreign tourists is still limited (although growing) so the quality of hotels is not as good as that offered in neighbouring countries for the same price.

Opening hours

Banks Mon-Fri 0900-1700, Sat 0900-1200, closed 29-30 Jun and 30-31 Dec.
Businesses Mon-Fri 0800-1200, 1400-1730; Sat 0800-1200.
Government offices Mon-Fri 0730-1530.

Post

Airmail to and from Europe can take up to a month, but is normally about 15 days; from the USA, 1 week. Certified packets to Europe cost US$9.25 per kilo and regular service is US$8.50 per kilo, good service; swifter, but more expensive, is **EMS** (US$34 per kg to Europe). Courier services are much quicker, but cost more. The correct address for any letter to the capital is 'San Salvador, El Salvador, Central America'.

Safety

Traditionally El Salvador has a reputation for violence and crime. In part this is a legacy of many years of civil war although this has been improved through a more active role of the police in later years. The reality is that most people visiting El Salvador return with reports of friendly, open people; far from being targeted by criminals, you are much more likely to receive a warm welcome and genuine interest in your visit. Locals will talk incessantly about the country's problems and dangers but few actual examples materialize. Be cautious until you find your own level of comfort and always ask local advice. Statistically El Salvador has the unenviable distinction of having the worst levels of violent crime on the continent. This derives from Salvadorean gang culture (*maras*) and most visitors will see nothing of this activity. If renting a car, buy a steering lock. Visitors to San Salvador should seek advice on where is not safe both inside and outside the city. For more on safety in the capital, see box, page 20.

Telephone

Country code T+503.
The **international direct dialling** code (to call out of El Salvador) is T00; 144+00 for **Telefónica**. There are no local area codes within El Salvador. There is a network of public phones for telecommunications companies – all use prepaid phone cards that only work in the company's particular machines. Available at most street corners,

supermarkets, gas stations to small shops they can be used for local and international calls, but make sure the card is from the same company as the public phone. The cards come in several denominations (US$1-3, US$5, US$10, US$25, etc). Mobile phones are very cheap. You can get a SIM card for US$3 and if you need a mobile phone you can get one from as little as US$12.

Some hotels will provide direct dialling – by far the easiest option. Dial T114 for **Information** (English spoken) and details of phone numbers in capital.

Time

- 6 hrs GMT.

Tipping

In upmarket restaurants: 10%, in others, give small change. Check your bill as most now add the 10% at the end (if they have, an additional tip is not needed). Nothing for taxi drivers except when hired for the day; airport porters, *boinas rojas* (red berets), US$2 per bag.

Tourist information

Corporación Salvadoreña de Turismo (**Corsatur**), at the Ministry of Tourism, Edificio Carbonel No1, Col Roma Alameda Dr Manuel Enrique Araujo Pasaje Carbonel San Salvador, T2243-7835; T2241-3200, www.elsalvador. travel. Provides information locally and on the web.
Revue, www.revuemag.com. English-language magazine published in Guatemala, with a section on El Salvador. Contains articles on places to visit and details of activities.

Useful websites

www.alfatravelguide.com Has a comprehensive listings of hotels throughout the country.

www.elsalvador.com Site of *El Diario de Hoy*– see 'Otros Sitios' for tourist info.

www.diariocolatino.com Site of the leftist *Co Latino* newspaper.

www.laprensa.com.sv Site of *La Prensa Gráfica* newspaper.

www.mipatria.net and **www.theother elsalvador.com** Access to useful information.

www.turismo.com.sv Lists of hotels, restaurants and interesting places to visit.

www.utec.edu.sv Site of Centre for Investigation of El Salvadorean Public Opinion (CIOPS) with information in Spanish on El Salvadorean political and social issues.

Visas and immigration

Every visitor must have a valid passport. No visas are required for European, US, Canadian, Australian or New Zealand nationals. The government website www.rree.gob.sv has a full list of country requirements.

Overstaying the limit on a tourist card can result in fines. Immigration officials can authorize up to 90 days' stay in the country; extensions may be permitted on application to Migración, Centro de Gobierno 9ª Calle Poniente y final 15 Avenida Norte, T2213-7778, Mon-Fri 0730-1530. As of 2006, when El Salvador signed a Central America-4 (CA-4) Border Control Agreement with Guatemala, Honduras and Nicaragua (see box, page 110), you have to visit a country outside of these 4 to re-enter and gain 90 days.

Weights and measures

The metric system is used alongside certain local units such as the *vara* (836 mm), *manzana* (7000 sq m) and the *quintal* (45 kg). Some US weights and measures are also used; US gallons are used for gasoline and quarts for oil.

Index → *Entries in bold refer to maps*

Credits

Footprint credits
Editor: Jo Williams
Production and layout: Emma Bryers
Maps: Kevin Feeney
Colour section: Angus Dawson

Publisher: Patrick Dawson
Managing Editor: Felicity Laughton
Administration: Elizabeth Taylor
Advertising sales and marketing:
John Sadler, Kirsty Holmes
Business Development: Debbie Wylde

Photography credits
Front cover: Stefano Ember/
Dreamstime.com. **Back cover**: Top:
Lana Bykova/Shutterstock.com. Bottom:
Fotos593/Shutterstock.com.

Colour section
Inside front cover: Milosz_M, Jan
Sochor/age fotostock, Christian
Kober/Robert Harding Picture Library,
Milosz_M. **Page 1**: Brizardh/Dreamstime.
com. **Page 2**: milosk50. **Page 4**: Stefano
Paterna/Alamy, Stefano Paterna/age
fotostock. **Page 5**: Brizardh/Dreamstime.
com, age fotostock/age fotostock,
Milosz_M/Shutterstock.com. **Page 6**:
imageBROKER/imageBROKER. **Page
7**: Animals Animals/Animals Animals.
Page 8: Florian Kopp/imagebro/
imageBROKER.
Duotone page 18: Stefano Ember/
Shutterstock.com

Printed in Spain by GraphyCems

Publishing information
Footprint El Salvador
2nd edition
© Footprint Handbooks Ltd
September 2015

ISBN: 978 1 909268 68 5
CIP DATA: A catalogue record for this
book is available from the British Library

® Footprint Handbooks and the
Footprint mark are a registered
trademark of Footprint Handbooks Ltd

Published by Footprint
6 Riverside Court
Lower Bristol Road
Bath BA2 3DZ, UK
T +44 (0)1225 469141
F +44 (0)1225 469461
footprinttravelguides.com

Distributed in the USA by
National Book Network, Inc.